Nights and Days in a Dark Carnival
Time Spent with Juggalos

By Craven Rock

Illustrations by Damon Thompson

Nights and Days in a Dark Carnival
Time Spent with Juggalos
Copyright © 2013 by Craven Rock

Illustrations Copyright © Damon Thompson

Mend My Dress Press
Tacoma, WA
MendMyDress.com

ISBN-13 978-0-9850131-8-9
Library of Congress Catalog-in-publication data availible upon request

These stories are based on events of the author's experiences, although some names have been changed for privacy reasons.

Acknowledgments

Thanks:
Ryan Bearcan, Joshua James Amberson, Alexis Wolf, Gina Siciliano, Chris Terry for editing help and putting up with me freaking out. Neelybat Chestnut and Colleen Twombly-Borst at Mend My Dress Press for putting this out and getting behind me. Kayla Greet for transcribing hours of Gathering interviews, may you never find the land of candy. Writing and moral support from my Mad & Manic friends Michele and Jordan, my Olytopia family, my Northwest Family and everybody who bugged me about it. KC, Kieran Harrison, Caleb Thompson and Jake Uitti and the rest of Monarch Review for all their support.

And of course, Damon Thompson for the adventure, ideas and illustrations.

This book is dedicated to the Juggalos with the best of intentions

Table of Contents

Nights and Days in a Dark Carnival

..the kingdom of Heaven suffereth violence
and the violent take it by force.
-Matthew 11:12

Yeah, everybody wear the mask, but how long will it last?
- The Fugees

I believe you can make forces of good and evil work for you,
to get what you want.
-G.G Allin

If you look for Cave-In-Rock on the map (that is, if anyone would bother to put it on a map), you would find it located in Southern Illinois—right where the state butts up against Indiana and Kentucky, an outpost where the Midwest meets the South, separated by the muddy Ohio River. It is the former home of indentured servants and horse thieves, passed down to their offspring who have been broken by construction work, disgraced by welfare, and mutated by meth; their stories and culture lost to landlessness and all the other indignities of the rural poor.

There, in August when the air, thick with humidity, leaves every alcoholic too worn out to even fuck or beat their wives, a gathering commences. For a former Hoosier, and former Kentuckian like myself, it's hard not to find it symbolic that this space is where the Gathering of the Juggalos takes place. But it is there where twenty thousand Juggalos come together for a family reunion of a subculture made up of mostly poor, disenfranchised, and uneducated followers of the horrorcore rap group, Insane Clown Posse.

I know this because I curiously watched the Juggalos for the past few years, and I plan on attending the next Gathering. I recruit an old buddy of mine, Damon, to come along as an illustrator and we spend four days mingling with this obscure and reclusive subculture. My obsession started a half-a-decade ago—I saw young people hanging on the streets of my neighborhood in Seattle with their faces painted up like evil clowns.

With more scrutiny, I noticed they were decked out in baggy T-shirts with a familiar logo I eventually recognize as Insane Clown Posse's (that clown rap band from the nineties) logo. At the time, I had no idea there was such a thing as Juggalos or Insane Clown Posse still existed as a band. But before I delve deeper into my Juggalo obsession, I'll start with what I knew at the time about the Juggalo idols: Insane Clown Posse (ICP).

I remember Insane Clown Posse as a duo of white rappers from Detroit, Violent J and Shaggy 2 Dope, who paint their faces like clowns with sharp and pointy edges to give them a leering, menacing countenance. They rapped about murder, mutilation and rape while they sprayed their audience down with Faygo, a generic soda brand from the Michigan area. Five or six years ago, this was all I could tell you about Insane Clown Posse. See, like a lot of people, I remembered how ICP worked their whole outrageous shtick at the same time Gothic band Marilyn Manson shock-rocked the mainstream with their dark industrial sound and androgynous stage show, but Insane Clown Posse had long since dropped under my radar and I had all but completely forgotten about them. As I continued to see teenagers riding the bus in full clown face paint, I had to look into it. I found out ICP hadn't faded away, but actually grew in popularity. This was partly due to the fact that instead of being a pop sensation they cleverly managed to build a mystique that provided them with a cult following. At the time of writing this, two of their albums have gone platinum and five gold, many charted in Billboard, and their most recent album, *Bang! Pow! Boom!*, debuted at #4 on the Billboard 200 and #1 on the Billboard Top Independent Albums charts. They managed to do all of this while being completely ignored by the mainstream media. They started a hugely successful label called Psychopathic Records, to which they've signed other rappers who also put on the clown makeup and rap, including Twiztid, Anybody Killa and Blaze Ya Dead Homie. Their collective success is entirely due to their "obsessive" fans called the Juggalos. Pop stars, rap stars and rock stars come and go, but the cult of the Wicked Clown continues to attract new followers and grow.

But why? What makes a band so completely unpopular to the mainstream (and even to underground rap fans) become such a huge cult phenomenon? How does a band whose inaccessible sound and aesthetics are so garish and off-putting continue to grow in popularity with young people when the artists themselves are in their late-thirties? What the fuck is this all about?

Their increasing popularity has a lot to do with their fans "getting it." Violent J and Shaggy 2 Dope, who make up Insane Clown Posse, are, in their own words, "the most hated band in the world" and have become successful by making their own dark and violent subgenre of rap music: Wicked Shit. All arguments for or against the quality and relevance of Wicked Shit aside, it's the evil darkness in the music that seems to attract one to become a Juggalo in the first place. From all the online research I compiled before my trip to the Gathering, I put together that Juggalos feel they're into something too edgy, too violent and too offensive for the rest of the world. Their love of Wicked Shit unites the Juggalos collectively into what they call the Juggalo Family. Only fellow Juggalos understand Wicked Shit and this strengthens the bond and solidarity between them, making them family. Kids who are already outcast and disenfranchised are no longer hated because they are too skinny, too fat, too ugly, too poor or too uneducated. They become Juggalos and are marginalized simply because they are too "wicked," too defiant, and too extreme.

> "Their recruiting rhetoric is a lot like skinheads,' Damon, my illustrator, says to me after doing some research before our trip, 'never being alone. Someone always having your back."

This is true, but being part of the "Fam" also carries with it the promise of "Clown Love." If one is "down with the Clown" they will get love from the Family—unconditionally. While there is a degree of unity and togetherness in any subculture, it seems much stronger in the Juggalo Family as there are fewer conditions and ethics to cause division amongst the fold, or at least more elusive and malleable ethics.

The ethics which guide the Juggalos are delivered to the Family by ICP on a series of albums called the Six Joker's Cards. Each of these albums reveal more and more of the Juggalo faith, also referred to as the Dark Carnival. According to Violent J, the Dark Carnival came to him in a vision. In the early nineties, when they called themselves the Inner City Posse, a gangsta rap group that was becoming popular in Detroit due to their own ceaseless promotion, Violent J experienced a vision—or what I might call a hallucination—of spirits and leering clowns, which lead to the Dark Carnival. He feels he was told by these spirit ninjas to spread the word of Dark Carnival on earth, and guide his followers in their path to reach Shangri-la, the afterlife of the Juggalos. (Confusingly, not only are Juggalos ICP fans, and followers of the faith known as the Dark Carnival, they are also collectively known as the Dark Carnival.)

In all my research on Insane Clown Posse and the Juggalos, one thing I never grasped is the Dark Carnival. It seems to be a chicken or the egg type of deal—I'm not sure if one knows they're a Juggalo because they instinctively pick up the spirituality in a bunch of songs about mutilation and serial killing, or if one forces themselves to cull something spiritual out of the lyrics because they feel the call to become a Juggalo. A layman like myself finds nothing in these songs but violence and dismemberment mixed in with scatological tales of jerking off in someone's mac-n-cheese. Whatever the Dark Carnival may entail, this spiritual awakening remains crucial to the Juggalo Family.

Carnival Gates

On the perfect night dead people get to sleep in
'cause when they wake up on a night like this its where to begin
The ringmaster's wagons can travel far and undisturbed
'cept they show up in the dark for the town they about to serve
-Shaggy 2 Dope

We leave Louisville, Kentucky, after dark, crossing over into Indiana. We're not too far before we're dipped completely in to the blackness of Highway 64, the only lights coming from the occasional Eastbound eighteen-wheeler. Fifteen miles over the border I see the truck stop sign near the exit leading to my teenage home, Milltown. My gut tightens as I think of that town—a town of meth and welfare and vicious brutality. When I left Milltown for Indianapolis, Insane Clown Posse were still Inner City Posse and just beginning to build up a rep in Detroit, and I was a punk rock kid with a poorly executed Mohawk and a chip on my shoulder. There weren't any Juggalos in Milltown then, I think to myself. My anxiety grows. Partially, it's fear of failure that eats at me; to come all the way out here and then to flop miserably at getting the Juggalo story. Maybe my anxiety has something to do with the Juggalo's reputation for violence, as well. Or it might just have something to do with passing the shitty small town that I grew up in, which is abstractly and subconsciously linked to my reason for making this trip.

There are no streetlights along the highway, just the long black Middle American rural night. So abysmal is the blackness that we're thankful for curves on the highway breaking the monotony, keeping sleep from sending us right off the road. All around us rural routes vein throughout the land leading to mobile homes and shacks where the forgotten live. If we drove down these gravel roads at any hour after dark, we would see lights in the windows, the residents inside wide awake, twitchy on crystal meth and guarded by Rottweilers and pit bulls and shotguns.

In the light of the dashboard Damon hits the search button on the radio dial. He's unusually cranky and silent as we drive, forced to leave on the fly after a bad day at work as a concierge. He leaves me alone to my thoughts as the country station—the only station for miles—fades out. The green LED numbers twirl, searching for another place to rest before finally stopping on a Classic Rock station. The cab fills with Axl Rose's trademark yowl ripping it's way through "Paradise City." The song, in context to location, brings back memories of Guns N' Roses blaring out of blown-out speakers of grey-primed hoopties as they ceaselessly cruised my old town until the engines finally gave up or the drivers drunkenly wrapped them around a tree.

How alienated I felt then; I desperately wanted out of there and wanted more. Living in such a fucked up place filled me with despair and desperation. Everything slides into context as I think about how I found punk rock and how it exposed me to everything good and healthy that would happen in my life. It empowered me, and politicized me, and provided an outlet for my anger at all of the fucked up things going on all around me. Punk rock ultimately taught me to fight for something—to do something more than knock somebody up and get stuck in a small town for the rest of my life. It all began by going out to my first punk rock show and feeling the energy of a room full of angry kids. It made me realize I wasn't so alone, like I could be a part of something.

That pissed-off energy from my youth makes me think of the ire punks and others in counter-culture exhibit towards the mere mention of Juggalos and I can't help feel it's a bit ironic. I too find the whole Juggalo aesthetic to be distasteful, from the sophomoric toilet humor of Wicked Shit to the eyesore aesthetics of HatchetGear (the Psychopathic Records clothing line) fashion. More importantly, on an ethical level, I'm grossed out by the materialism, misogyny and anti-intellectualism prevalent in Juggalo culture. But I can't help empathize with the Juggalos. If I don't understand what Juggalos do, I think I can understand why they do it, and maybe it's this empathy that led me to come all the way out here. Or maybe I'm just waxing pretention as I ride down I-64, forced to confront my past. Maybe it's just the oddness and esoteric nature of Juggalo culture I want figure out, to get a grasp and put some closure on a long obsession. Maybe I just want to give them a fair shake, something they rarely, if ever, receive. Insane Clown Posse is wealthy and successful enough to be treated with some respect every now and then, but the Juggalos rarely get anything but hate outside of the Dark Carnival.

After four hours of driving and another hour of getting lost, we find the obscure dirt road leading to Hogrock, the alleged biker-owned land where the Gathering takes place. It's three o'clock in the morning when we finally pull in. The Gathering looks like a mutated, nightmarish state fair. There is a carnival midway where one can buy staples like elephant ears, corn dogs and Jumbo Bitch Beaters (Juggalo for a large turkey leg). There are carnival games that no one seems to be playing and near the Main Stage there is a Ferris Wheel and a rocket ride called the Saturn 6.

Tents are strewn haphazardly everywhere in the Big Baller campsites. Big Baller campsites include electricity and running water. They cost a few hundred dollars (not included in the ticket price), as opposed to the free camping in the parking lot outside the grounds where we're camped, but the Juggalos cut the cost down by overflowing each spot with all their friends. Big Baller sites aren't marked, reserved or designated; instead it's pay per vehicle. So one group of Juggalos pays to drive a vehicle in stake out land, and then all their homies will park outside, walk in to the grounds and stake tents all around the paying friends' tent to split up the cost. This makes for a chaotic and boundless tent city, symbolic of the resourcefulness, as well as the devil-may-care-attitude of the Juggalos.

Some Juggalos are running around with glow sticks strapped all over themselves. Some are decked out in full Wicked Clown face paint. Even the entertainment is similar to a state fair line-up—washed up groups from over ten years ago like Naughty By Nature and Above The Law. In the Freak Tent a band called Critical Bill plays really bad yo-metal that sounds as if it came out of a time warp from the mid-nineties. For non-musical entertainment, we can choose between big-dicked porn star, Ron Jeremy, doing stand-up comedy, or the premier of *Big Money Rustlas,* a Western movie made by Insane Clown Posse. It looks like any other Western, only Shaggy 2 Dope and Violent J's characters are done up in their clown makeup, while the rest of the cast just wears John Wayne-esque garb.

My feet nearly get run over by a golf cart as I distractedly sip on my beer. A chorus of "WHOOP! WHOOP!" goes up from the three seated Juggalos in the cart and four hanging off the back. A sign on the back says "rides $3.00 or tits" and these carts constantly zigzag through the grounds, even during the late hours.

> "Hey ninja," I hear over my shoulder from a chubby female Juggalo in full face paint, as I recover from my near handicapping.

> "Have you seen my Juggalette around here? Wearing a short skirt with big titties?" She asks.

Thus my first conversation begins with a Juggalo after all of these years of armchair internet research.

> "Nah, I didn't. I'm sure that I'd notice something like that," I reply, looking away awkwardly.

> "C'mon, ninja, you got them glasses on and shit," she teases dryly.

> "Hey, y'all got the same shorts," Damon cuts in and laughs.

> "Why you bitin' my style?" She wanders off in the other direction.

We cross the didactically named Drug Bridge to get to the Second Stage. Drug Bridge is 20 yards long and a couple of cars wide, and on it is a scene like no other—under streetlights dizzy with moths Juggalos ball every kind of drug imaginable…every kind of drug. Juggalos hock them fearlessly while using incriminating terms. Ecstasy. Cocaine. Ketamine. Xanax. Percocet. A lot of the dealers can't possibly be older than sixteen. They hold signs made out of cardboard ripped from Faygo boxes and marked "Purple Kush $25," "Acid $10 a hit," and "Rolls $10." There are at least 60 people on the bridge—selling, buying or just milling about socializing. The dealers all shout out what they have and it's a cacophonous din, reminding me of the sound of street vendors in Mexican markets, but even more disorderly. This lawlessness is one benefit to the Gathering being on private property—as long as the cops aren't called, the Juggalos manage to get away with anything.

Across the Drug Bridge and in the area called Scrub Central, we see the Second Stage where Afroman, a flash-in-the-pan from the early 2000's sings his odes to pot and tall cans. Some of the crowd happily shout out the chorus to "I Got High," while others launch water balloons at him. He's getting Clown Love.

A Juggalo near me chucks a plastic bottle at the stage and a mustached guy in a yellow jacket shines a Maglite on him. I take him to be Afroman's own personal security because he is the only security I see all week besides those guarding ICP when on the main stage. The Juggalo then gets his own flashlight and shines it in the yellow-jacketed man's face for the rest of the set, and the security guard grows angrier while the Juggalo and his crew laugh at him. It's a clear representation of who holds the power at the Gathering and helps ground me to where I'm going to be for the next four days. Lawlessness is the rule.

After Afroman's set, we cross back over the Drug Bridge and a guy decked out in HatchetGear shouts out, "five dollar lines of coke!" His crew, also wearing HatchetGear, surround him.

Damon reaches in my backpack, which contains only toilet paper and tall cans of beer, grabs the T.P. and makes a stop at the third in a long line of spray-painted port-a-potties. I notice the phrase "namaste sharts" in red paint as the door closes.

"Somebody shit in the urinal," he says when he comes back out.

Miracle at Hogrock

We don't have to be high to look in the sky/ And know that's a miracle opened wide/Look at the mountains, trees, the seven seas/ And everything chilling underwater, please/ Hot lava, snow, rain and fog/ Long neck giraffes, and pet cats and dogs.
-Insane Clown Posse

Insane Clown Posse went viral not long ago and gained quite a bit of notoriety. Haters poke fun at the video for their song "Miracles," an anti-intellectual, quasi-Christian homage to nature, in which Violent J and Shaggy 2 Dope gush with the rapture of a couple of blissed-out E-tards about stuff like long-necked giraffes, "fucking rainbows and dirt," and proclaim them miracles. At one point Shaggy asks, "fucking magnets, how do they work?" before boldly stating "and I don't wanna talk to a scientist, y'all motherfuckers lyin' and gettin' me pissed."

One could defend the song as an embrace of childlike wonder rather than an ode to stupidity, but either way, it's a ridiculous song—so ridiculous that it received millions of hits on Youtube based on mockery alone. Prior to the music video attention, Saturday Night Live parodied an internet infomercial Insane Clown Posse and Psychopathic Records made promoting the 10th Gathering of the Juggalos. The 15 minute SNL skit promoted an absurd, trashy rock festival promising a guy being shot out of a cannon three times a day, dudes on stilts and ninjas spinning fire, a wrestling event called Bloodymania 3, real midway games and "plenty of food all over that bitch for all the hungry-asses out there," as well as lots of outhouses, wet T-shirt contests, Pauly Shore, and helicopter rides. Saturday Night Live's parody was a noble effort, but even though they went as far as to promote a helicopter spraying piss on the attendees, fact proves to be far more surreal. The skit was way more successful at drawing attention to the Juggalo Family than Insane Clown Posses' actual infomercial.

Part of the subculture's intrigue is the fact it's growing and getting stronger, not fading out like fads do. Nor has it lost the appeal to young people as Violent J and Shaggy push forty. All of the negative mainstream attention was bound to happen because the Juggalos were just getting too big to ignore.

"Oh my God, I have to see those titties," A Juggalo pleads from the back of the Love Wagon to a well-endowed, thick Juggalette as it passes by.

She smiles shyly, looks to the right to her Juggalette friend and then down at the ground. The Love Wagon is basically a hay ride without the hay—a huge wood and metal trailer pulled by a John Deere tractor with about 30-plus Juggalos hanging all over it at any given time.

Damon gets nailed with a Faygo bottle hucked by one of the riders and we hear a chorus of "WHOOP! WHOOP!" He laughs, chucks it back and we continue walking back to camp for more beer.

"Nice shirt," a guy sitting on a picnic table with his girlfriend says to Damon about his Misfits T-shirt, which already created a small controversy here. Some compliment him on it, but most give him shit for liking something other than Wicked Shit.

"Thanks, want a beer?" Damon asks them.

"Sure, if you can spare one," he says, and I sigh to myself.

"I'm Nathan," he says, then shakes our hands.

The girl introduces herself as Samantha. They both look a little bit like indie rockers—Samantha has long blonde hair, blue eyes and wears a vintage sun dress complimented by home-crafted jewelry. Nathan's well-shaven and has short black hair. He wears a pastel blue T-shirt of an obscure band and blue jeans that fit. They aren't wearing HatchetGear, but what really makes them stand out is they're a gorgeous couple, by anybody's standards.

"We're from Portland," Nathan says.

"Which one?" I ask.

They're from Portland, Oregon. Nathan is the reason they're here. He's one of a rare breed–an Insane Clown Posse fan (but not a Juggalo). Nathan used to be really into ICP in his teens and still holds a soft spot for them, so they came all this way to see his old faves and to check out the craziness. We walk together; Damon's in one of his drunken raconteur moods, and by the time we arrive back at the van they're enthralled by tales of his anti-racist skinhead past and how he used to thump Nazis back in the day.

I follow Damon to the back of the van when he heads to the cooler.

"Get rid of them," I whisper to him.

If he hears me he doesn't acknowledge it. I like them, but I imagine us just talking to the non-Juggalos we meet out here and I want to avoid other outsiders. I only want to talk to Juggalos. I want to get into the Juggalo mind-set and just talk to the Family. We've already been approached by a journalist and a photographer who are here together. Like Nathan, they broke the ice with Damon's Misfits T-shirt. They wear press passes and are the real thing, but we want to stay scrubby.

I guess Nathan and Samantha are in their early twenties. Folks their age tend to find the Juggalos less bizarre or less mysterious for the simple fact they went to high school with some of them. It's really fascinating to think there might be a whole lunch table of Juggalos in some high schools now; when I was in high school there weren't enough misfits to fill one table, let alone a whole crew claiming allegiance to one band.

If Nathan ever considered himself a Juggalo he doesn't let on. What's relevant at this stage in his life is he's an un-ironic fan. He and Samantha drove all the way across the country to see this. Hell, these two are probably even crazier and weirder than we are to be out here—at least we're not out here for entertainment. But entertained they are! They laugh when they tell us some of the things they've seen. They have a detached point of view, but aren't necessarily condescending. I don't let Damon know, but

I'm glad to have met them. Later on, after the Gathering ended, I wonder what they do in Portland, what music they listen to now, what the hell they're all about, and if I'll ever run into them again.

Once again, Damon made the right move. Getting to know Nathan and Samantha allows us to hear about some of the crazy stuff we'll miss at the Gathering since we can't be everywhere at once. But I don't tell them I'm here to write about it.

Except for Nathan and Samantha, and the journalist and his photographer, we have yet to encounter another non-Juggalo. There may be a few journalists running around exploiting their backstage passes, but out here it seems there are 20,000 Juggalos and us. I take a whole lot of comfort in this. Due to all the hype about the "Miracles" video, I was expecting we might already be behind the curve and the Gathering would be overrun with ironic hipster bloggers. But it's not, and this gives me some peace of mind about our project. It also makes me feel more adventurous.

"Fuck it!" I think to myself tossing my ancient tape recorder into the van. The damn thing is pretty much broken and at this point I'm kind of drunk, another example of how fly-by-night this project is. I come back around to where Damon sits, he looks at me and just busts out laughing.

> "Dude, you don't fit in here at all,' he laughs, 'With that ridiculous hat, the journal pouch on your belt and your glasses and your shoes... Dude, nobody here is wearing Converse."

> "Fuck you," I say, smile, and throw my hat into the van with dramatized frustration.

I grab the tape recorder again. It's at least been working some of the time and we head back inside the gates.

Damon's and my plan was to throw proper journalism to the wind and just do what the Juggalos do—to meet folks, possibly make friends and to avoid the detached distance other journalists approach their subjects with. Getting drunk is something that we both spend a lot of time doing anyway, when we're not working on our craft, and sometimes even when we are. We may not do everything the Juggalos do, but this one's easy.

Wanting to start somewhere with my questions for the Juggalos, I decide the Dark Carnival is a good place. I figure I'll ask them what the Dark Carnival means to them, and see where it goes from there. I've got a healthy buzz but I'm not totally shit-faced. I'm with my best friend in the world and the sun is going down and the air is still thick with grape blunts. A sweet smell I'm sure will forever trigger the Gathering for me. I feel positive as we walk; it's as good a starting point as any.

I start thinking about Damon and how glad I am to have him along. His coming was an accident, but possibly one of the only things that I did right in my preparation. I only called Damon to tell him that I was going to be flying into Louisville soon on my way to the Gathering of the Juggalos, and asked him jokingly,

"Wanna go?"

"No,' he said firmly, 'of course I don't want to go."

I could hear the laughter of some of his friends in the background. I laughed then asked,

"What if I paid?" Still joking.

"Maybe. If you paid," he said.

I hung up the phone and thought about it. Damon would be the perfect guy to take with me. I called him the next day and he actually agreed to come.

First of all, my purpose for bringing him would be as my illustrator, but he came in handy a lot of other ways. For instance—basic safety—I had no clue what I was getting myself into or what it would be like. While it could all be just a lot of hype, Juggalos have a reputation for being violent. Not being at the Gathering totally alone was definitely something to take into consideration. I went from having to hitchhike out to the middle of nowhere, then trying to figure how to camp with just a backpack without getting all my shit stolen, to riding in a van with my best friend and having someone to run around and get drunk with and to bounce observations off of. It's a hell of a lot better than wandering around by myself, awkwardly trying to mingle.

Besides, we're really comfortable around each other, and that makes other people comfortable around us. Damon is an easy, fun guy to be around, he's an enormous brawler, but he's also good at listening to people, reading them and respecting them. He doesn't suffer fools lightly, but he genuinely struggles to respect the flawed animal that is humanity, in spite of how much it conflicts with his cunning intelligence.

I could go on about the complexities of Damon, but overall, I couldn't ask for a better companion out here, except for the fact that he's struggling with intense pain in his left foot. This changes the game a bit, and I spend a lot of time running around taking things in by myself. When he gets back from the Gathering he finds out that he has gout, a disease that is triggered and escalated by heavy drinking.

Wicked Shit 101

The more haters you have in your life, the fresher you are.
-Violent J

To understand the nuances of Juggalo life, it may be a good idea to explore the subtle differences in the music they listen to—Wicked Shit and horrorcore. First of all, Wicked Shit and horrorcore are similar. They both use gory and macabre imagery–lyrics of stabbings, beheadings and if-you-fuck-with-me-I'll-brutally-murder-you themes. Horror films strongly influence both. However, they are not synonymous; all Wicked Shit can be called horrorcore, but not all horrorcore can be called Wicked Shit. Horrorcore is much less of a cult phenomenon than Wicked Shit and exists more as a subgenre of hip-hop than a scene that stands alone. Well-respected and critically-acclaimed MC's and producers have associated with horrorcore. For instance, Dr. Octagon (aka Kool Keith's) *Dr. Octagonecologyst* is considered by many a classic hip-hop album, but few would think of it as a horrorcore record, even though Keith does and has gone as far as saying he invented the style. Also Prince Paul and RZA were part of the horrorcore group Gravediggaz, long after making their names in hip-hop.

Wicked Shit, from my narrow understanding, is made by and for the Juggalos. Basically, one expects some Wicked Clown involvement (or at least a huge tolerance for greasepaint) with anything dubbed Wicked Shit. More than likely a group playing Wicked Shit clowns up on stage and alludes to the Dark Carnival and Shangri-la in their lyricism. Wicked Shit is a term used almost exclusively by the Juggalos. It can also be argued that Wicked Shit is religious or spiritual music, because generally it teaches the way of the Dark Carnival. If anyone blends the two terms Wicked Shit and horrorcore it is usually the Juggalos, not fans of horrorcore.

I find the Juggalos level of Puritanism baffling. A large portion of Juggalos only listen to Psychopathic Records bands, but there are also Juggalos who branch out to the larger horrorcore. Some even get behind everything and everyone Violent J and Shaggy 2 Dope endorse, including, for instance, a lot of the old 90's acts at the Gathering like Vanilla Ice and Naughty By Nature. I don't get to talk to every Juggalo about their personal taste in music, but I meet many who claim to like classic rock and maybe some alternative stuff. Overall it seems they don't branch too far out from Wicked Shit. For instance, the occasional shit Damon gets for his Misfits T-shirt may not be because Juggalos think The Misfits are a shitty band, but because it's not Wicked Shit. This isolationism comes down from the leadership of ICP. Even though they're total hip-hop heads themselves and that's why they rap, they give something entirely different to the Juggalos with Wicked Shit. With Wicked Shit, the Dark Carnival and the Juggalo Family, ICP are able to isolate the Juggalos from anything else. As a result, Juggalos may feel stronger as a group while also feeling like they're too subversive, underground and profane for the masses to understand. By enclosing the virtues of ICP within their Family, the Juggalos continue to build a mythology amongst themselves that their music is too fucked up or wicked for the rest of the world and the haters, rather than being merely corny or dumb. The dark and violent style which ICP chooses to play works to this advantage, ICP benefits greatly from the Juggalos' seclusion, and are able to further manipulate their niche market into buying merchandise and supporting their tours.

This isolationism also informs my fascination with the Juggalos. They exist in a cultural vacuum—either mocked or ignored by the rest of rap culture, which they gloat only makes them stronger. In addition to this, they are cut off from counter-cultural lineage altogether. As much as the different affiliations within modern subculture may not get along smoothly, they all come from a long thread of resistance. Punk said, "never trust a dirty hippie" but it was a reaction against the stoned, drop-out culture the 60's hippie movement turned into. At heart punk and hippie shared a lot of the same ethics. How far it goes back is not something that I care to get into here, but the style and fashion of counter-culture, from hip-hop, to punk, to the black-clad anarchists, each carry their own cultural alchemy, all of which is linked to something else. The Wicked Clown aesthetic doesn't trigger this alchemy or this historical memory of resistance, resulting in coming across as garish and repulsive to the rest of counter-culture. For example, I may have vastly different taste than some of my raver friends who listen to electronic music, but we can come together under an umbrella of radicalism or D.I.Y politics. The Juggalo in the clown makeup stands alone...with his Family.

This helps explain why the Juggalos are such a shock and a mystery to the rest of counter-culture. Juggalos gross out punks, they offend or induce pity from anarchists and radicals, hipsters make fun of them, and the rest of hip-hop pretends they don't exist. But none of these groups actually know any Juggalos and they remain a mystery to all these groups. In my short time at the Gathering I develop a bit of sympathy for the Juggalos. In spite of my snobbishness towards their overall aesthetic and revulsion at their sexism, materialism and conformity, I feel that they came to the Family for the same reason that anyone would join any subculture–to be empowered.

I wake up when it starts to get hot in the van. It's early in the morning and already muggy. Damon has been up and wandering around and now he draws in the front seat of the van; he turns around and shows me the picture.

"Look what I saw this morning,' he says with a grin, 'a bunch naked girls hanging off the back of a golf cart."

He sets his sketchbook down, we grab a jug of water and head back out into the madness.

It doesn't take long for us to ease into the Gathering. Looking around at the crowd, I feel less intimidated than I did on the way in. Most look like the same crustached and goateed poor white folks that I grew up around, except they are decked out in HatchetGear. As Damon bluntly puts it, "They've managed to bring together the redneck and the wigger." I may have left those shitty towns that my family lived in far behind, but I remember the desperate need for dignity that causes folks there to lash out in bursts of what is considered random violence by people who refuse to understand or respect them. A phrase comes to mind, one I've often heard repeated in jest by the non-Juggalo–"don't fuck with a Juggalo." But let me say, at the risk of watering down the drama or making our mission seem less intrepid, we've encountered little trouble out here because we've shown respect.

We pass several camps as we walk the trail. Homemade banners display where each party hails from, bedsheets bare names like Grimtown, VA, Camp Chaos and Bay Area Ninjas in permanent marker, surrounded by logos of Wicked Shit bands and Insane Clown Posse's ubiquitous Hatchetman logo, a cartoonish silhouette of a dreadlocked man running with a hatchet. There are also plenty of professionally done banners people shelled out quite bit for, just for some hometown pride. Beat-up cars covered in Psychopathic Records stickers litter the grounds along with rented RVs. Every now and then we see a customized hot rod or lowrider—sleek, glittery and proudly proclaiming Wicked Clown affiliation with their design. Most of the camps sell cans of Faygo, hot dogs, glow sticks, glow-in-the-dark hatchets, loosies (single cigarettes), shots of whiskey, Jell-o shots, or cans of beer. Scrawled cardboard signs advertising these wares hang on poles and trees around each camp. Unlike a punk fest or hippie gathering, and true to their hip-hop roots, out here it's all balls-out hustling. Everyone is doing it. Some Juggalos even thought as far ahead to bring things like batteries and bags of ice to sell at a profit. The Juggalos are generally pretty fair, though; cans of beer don't go for much more than a dollar. It's laissez faire capitalism combined with a respect for Family.

The sweet scent of blunts, carnival food and the loud call and response of "WHOOP! WHOOP!" permeate the humid air. "WHOOP! WHOOP!' is the cry of the Juggalo. They use it to convey many things: they shout it out as greeting, they shout it out when they're drunk, they shout it out when they're high and they shout it out to let everyone know that they're a down-ass 'lo having a good time. Exactly how important the chant is becomes clear at about 10:00 AM on our first morning as we walk through Spazzmatic.

Spazzmatic acts as a bar/social area, a sort of cabana where picnic tables surround a wooden bar behind which a chunky Juggalette serves nothing but Faygo and a few snacks. Hiding in the shade from the blazing sun, Juggalos kick it on the picnic tables, catching up on the last year and talking about representing the Hatchet in their town. When we walk in, a scraggly goateed, long-haired white kid, shirtless and wearing HatchetGear basketball shorts, sticks out his fist to give me knucks. I give him his dap and he grins. As we move through the tables, Juggalos continue to converse amongst each other like any bar or party or lunchroom scenario, except every couple of minutes someone calls out "WHOOP! WHOOP!" and the whole vicinity answers back, "WHOOP! WHOOP!" Then they turn back to their conversations. A few minutes later it happens again. "WHOOP! WHOOP!" We quickly work this phrase into our vocabulary.

A common chant besides "WHOOP! WHOOP!" is "FAMILY!" Each syllable pronounced with deep-throated inflection so it comes out, "FAM-UH-LEE!" Hearing large groups of Juggalos echo it all around reminds me that I don't belong here and unsettles me. There's a non-verbal Juggalo signifier in their hand sign, a complicated twisting of their fingers into what I finally figure out is supposed to be "W.C." for the Wicked Clown.

A proper way to greet a Juggalo or a Juggalette (a female Juggalo) is to say the shortened "'lo" or "'lette", but there's also "ninja," as in, "what up, ninja?" At first, I thought this might be a way for a white rap group to put a twist on "nigga" without perpetrating, but according to Violent J, it just came out of him and Shaggy's childhood love of Kung-Fu movies. A whole lot of their aesthetics are based off things they were into as kids—wrestling, the macabre, the occult, and Faygo soda, to list a few. Since they found success at a young age, they didn't need to give up a lot of their childhood obsessions.

Juggalo street wear closely resembles 90's hip-hop style—baseball and basketball jerseys, oversize T-shirts and basketball shorts, everything baggy and loose. Around their necks they wear the large gaudy amulet of the Hatchetman, the most common logo of Insane Clown Posse. What obviously stands out is nearly all of the mentioned articles bear some kind of Wicked Shit logo and about eighty-percent of Juggalos here sport a logo of artists represented by Psychopathic Records at all times. If we count tattoos the number of logos jumps over ninety-percent.

While hairstyles of the Juggalo vary greatly—from colored hair and mohawks to short, cropped hair and shaved heads. A signature Juggalo haircut is two rows of braided hair like the kind Coolio wore in the nineties. The guys usually rock a few days stubble or the common goatee.

Juggalettes often wear the same style as the boys as far as the baggy clothes, but more often they let it all hang out, wearing next to nothing. Less common are the Juggalettes in bright colors with fluorescent hair extensions, platform boots and glowsticks around their necks, a look resembling ravers or club kids. This is a controversial look and the 'lettes who dress like this tell me they take some shit for looking like ravers. I also see a lot baggy pants with lots of the zippers and chains and straps hanging off of them, and here, just like anywhere else, teenagers usually sport this style, and not older Juggalos.

The ages of Juggalos range widely, and although most of them are teenagers or in their early twenties, we see a lot of Juggalos that are in their thirties or forties or even older.

I'd estimate at least a quarter to a third of the Juggalos are women. Most of them prefer the title Juggalette, yet some demand to be called Juggalos. ICP claims the term Juggalette was coined because of an angry feminist somewhere who complained about the lack of a term for women, but they think both genders have a right to the term Juggalo. The idea of feminists forcing a group to apply the suffix "-ette" to anything sounds absurd, as to my knowledge, feminists have almost succeeded in putting an end to the condescending suffix altogether. Nonetheless, when Googling "Juggalo + feminist," most of what comes up is angry female Juggalos who reject the term Juggalette and are upset ICP felt coerced to use the term.

In spite of having this representation of women, a whole lot of the entertainment at the Gathering is based around their objectification. Faygo wet T-shirt contests. Oil wrestling. Things of that nature. Matter of fact, degrading women seems to be the rule and no one of any gender seems to have a problem with it.

One myth of the Juggalo quickly dispelled by our time at the Gathering is Juggalos are white. While I didn't completely buy into that assumption, the percentage of People of Color at the Gathering surprises me. At least 20% of those attending seem to be Black or African-American people, Latinos, and Native Americans, proving the Juggalo Family extends beyond the white trash and suburbanite stereotype. In contrast to any other subculture I've experienced, the Family is far and away the most diverse.

It's my own prejudice and preconceptions about People of Color, but I figured mostly white people were attracted to the Family because poor, white folks don't have the same identity politics that one often finds in communities of People of Color or queer communities. I feel some shock at seeing Black people wearing the clown makeup and I'm forced to look at stereotypes I've bought into about Black people always having to be "cool."

Taking this further, the scapegoating of the Juggalos may be another way for the wealthy to play up stereotypes of the poor and minorities. I don't realize while at the Gathering, but a photographer from one of Seattle's alternative weeklies also came out cover the story. She's photographed the Juggalos in my town for a while now, catching them outside ICP shows and posing them in front of dumpsters overflowing with garbage. Seattle, being a wealthy city, yucked it up over these photos and the paper's web-page scrolled down endlessly with dehumanizing comments. The hatred of Juggalo culture is integral to its growth and strength. However, the reporter only stays out here two days, photographing late at night, after the sun goes down on the 105 degree days, and the 'los are well-lit and partying hard during the only four days a year that they get to spend with their Family. She photographs them topless, covered in mud and standing in front of port-a-potties with clown makeup smeared and in disarray; capturing them bleary-eyed, clutching bags of Ecstasy and giant buds of weed.

Whether or not photographing the Juggalos in this manner exploitative is arguable, seeing as the wasted Juggalos posed for these photographs, but I am shocked at how one-sided they appear. The photos don't show Juggalos grilling and sharing food or waiting in line for the nasty showers, nor do they show tender Juggalo lovers or, hell, just Juggalos chilling out together simply having a good time. She covers the Juggalos here like she always covers them, from a detached standpoint of bourgeoisie bohemian schadenfreude. It makes me sick to see a young, probably well-educated (I guess I stereotype, too), hip photojournalist come this far to portray the Juggalos in such a way without even the slightest interest in under-standing why it's happening. She brags online about how her crew didn't blend in with their Slayer T-shirts and how she feared getting her camera stolen, implying courage, yet it seems to me she barely dipped a toe in the Gathering or the Juggalo culture.

Another inaccuracy in her photo series brings me back to the event's ethnicity. In the forty-six piece photo series she only captured five visible People of Color. It feels subconsciously intentional. In these "post-racial" times, the privileged continue to find sneaky ways to lash out at the underclass and reinforce stereotypes. I don't know the photographer's background or story, but alternative and hipster types have recently targeted the Juggalos as an outlet for their displaced class prejudice. The mainstreaming of Juggalo mockery can be interpreted as a slippery way of laughing at poverty in a way that distances the hip from they're own smug, elitism; a way of saying "Look, I'm into cool shit and they're painting themselves up in clown faces and listening to horrible music."

The People of Color represented in the photos are dressed more conservatively, in common street clothes with less face paint and HatchetGear. Two of the five are Black male performers on stage dressed in hip-hop attire, possibly not even Wicked Shit rappers, but simply an act booked for the Gathering. Possibly the idea of Black people being at the Gathering, worshiping ICP and painting themselves up conflicts with a stereotype of Black people being the purveyors of cool or perhaps reflects a fetishism of People of Color's rise up from oppression. Maybe the alternative, leisure class prefers to continue the stereotype that white people have no excuse for being poor, uneducated and trashy and worthy of being mocked and laughed at for their position. In the end, the series of photographs reveals the familiar face of race and class oppression, but now the leisure class doesn't even have to poke fun at white trash. Now they have the Juggalos.

Floobs and Scrubs

I was born, first, they threw me in a shit pile
I dealt with it, and lived there for a while
I got dissed on, pissed on, and beat down
Mutilated, and tossed out a dead clown
Next thing ya know, I'm chillin' at the big top
Free money, and mad bitches non-stop
No water, it's Faygo on tap
-Violent J

"The only other thing I remember about my real dad, Rick, was him throwing a TV set at my mom. She was standing at the bottom of the stairs, and he was at the top. She had to pull me out of the way as it came crashing down." recounts Violent J, of one of his earliest memories from the age of two. Afterwards, his father took off, swiping his and J's moms savings from her hand, never to be seen again.

Thus began Joe Bruce (aka Violent J)'s childhood with his brother, Rob Bruce, and their sister, Theresa. From then on a revolving door of seemingly sociopathic stepfathers and boyfriends who humiliated, degraded and physically abused them, and even kicked their dog around, entered their lives. He tells these stories in his autobiography, *ICP: Behind the Paint*, in laid back way, but the wounds still come across as raw.

He also tells a story about a horrible baby-sitter who locked them in an empty backyard on the days their mother worked. They cherished moments when the neighbor dog dug through the fence to play with them. At times, the baby-sitter's own kids came into the backyard. "I hated playing with them. See, they had this fucked-up habit of unzipping their pants and waggling their dicks at us, then chasing us around like that." J's mother knew they were unhappy, he says, "If we complained... all she'd say was 'there's nothing I can do about it; I don't know who else to get.' She was telling the truth, there really was nobody else." The level of desperation in this statement deeply illuminates the reality of the hardship this single-mother family of four went through.

As kids who experienced hell at home, they often got little relief in school where the Bruce brothers were "legendary scrubs." They were often in debt to their school, owing lunch money and their names were announced over the PA, letting everyone know they couldn't pay. "If you step on a cracked tile, you gotta kiss one of the Bruce Brothers." was a phrase girls said around school.

The Juggalos respect Violent J's rough childhood because the Juggalos are outcasts too. I guess that's where I come in. I feel compassion for the Juggalos because I was an outcast at school, too. I never owned the right clothes in middle school and high school, my family struggled financially and there was a lot of shit going on at home. More importantly, my family took a serious dive, we moved from being a middle-class family in Bismarck, North Dakota to a financially struggling family in a rough, white, working class town right outside of Gary, Indiana. To make it worse, I had been home-schooled for years by my Pentecostal mother. My only outside exposures being a church youth group and other weird, freak, home-school kids. When we moved to Indiana, I was thrown into a violent junior high in the middle of the year. I had no idea how things worked, no social skills, weighed about eighty pounds and was years away from puberty. I had so little world experience that if kids asked me if I was jacking off, I honestly didn't know. I was fucked. I sat completely alone in the cafeteria every day. I'm not saying this to piggy-back, or in any way say I had it as bad as Violent J, but to state why I feel for the Juggalos. I know how important it is to find a place where you fit—I'm still trying to do it. It's also probably why I root for the underdog. But this isn't about me and spineless, vague statements about my past like "there was a lot of shit going on at home," it's about the Juggalos. It's not about ICP or Violent J, but the Juggalos follow him militantly, so to understand the Juggalos we need to look at Violent J and why his influence is successful.

Baudelaire once said, "Genius is nothing more nor less than childhood recaptured at will." and if anybody's nailed that action, it's Violent J. He epitomizes escape, a tactic that not only saved him as a child, but is a cornerstone of Psychopathic Records' empire and the core of his own success. By escape, I mean the obsessions that he, his brother, Rob, and later Joe (who would become Shaggy 2 Dope) used to escape the real world and to cope, obsessions that became keys to their success.

Some of these obsessions include:

1. **Wrestling and ninja movies.** They were so obsessed with these genres they started their own backyard wrestling leagues as teenagers. Kung-Fu theater influenced them to started calling each other "ninja." Both these childhood consequences stuck with them into adulthood, up to the point where they wrestled as Insane Clown Posse in major federations and eventually started their own Juggalo Class Wrestling.

2. **Hip-hop.** Violent J and Shaggy discovered rap early in their pre-teens. They started hip-hop crews inspired by Run-DMC and UTFO and even went through phases of graffiti and break-dancing.

3. **The Supernatural.** Violent J strongly believes he is in tune to spiritual worlds and never faltered in the belief. It started when he and his brother Rob saw God. According to a story in his biography, their mom went out of town for a week and left them fifty dollars for food, and they were stoked to spend it all on stuff like chips and dip and pizza. But the neighborhood bully found out about it and intimidated them into letting him stay the night; he ate all of their chips and dip and ruined everything. That is, until J and Rob saw God. Both of them saw a black hooded figure coming up the stairs and they knew it was God showing them everything was going to be OK, in spite of the bully fucking up their night. It's my favorite part of Violent J's book because even as an adult it has this tone of "ha ha, the mean ol' bully didn't get to see God coming up the stairs." He continued to have these supernatural experiences, eventually leading to the Dark Carnival.

4. **Floob Pride.** Another thing they all carried over from the pain of their childhood was the concept of being a "floob" or a "scrub." Violent J and Rob owned this, said "fuck it!" and began taking pride in being poor and trashy. They proudly rode their shitty Huffys while other kids rode Diamondbacks and Mongooses and even asked their mother to pull right up in front of the school to drop them off in her beat-up hooptie. They said "fuck it" to school and education. They slacked off and wrestled and

did petty crime instead. Violent J tells these stories with as much conviction as Malcolm X tells of his education and enlightenment. And why not? It's his story. It worked for him. Whatever the Juggalos have gone through or might be going through, Violent J suffered something similar. He and his brother took the names they were called—"floob" and "scrub"—back. They started calling themselves these names, claiming them for their own. When Violent J grew up he threw them into the Juggalo mix. The Juggalos were the kids that didn't fit in. They were the fat kids, the ugly kids and the poor kids. Proud floobs! Juggalos!

These Islands

If I only could, I'd set the world on fire.
Say, FUCK THE WORLD! FUCK THE WORLD!
-Insane Clown Posse

An obese middle-aged Juggalo, shirtless and tattooed in Psychopathic designs, tells me the heat index is up to 110 degrees. It's still morning.

"Stay hydrated," he says.

The sweltering temperature is supposed to continue for the rest of the Gathering—heavy, sticky heat that makes one want to just lay around all day. The sun shines bright and high overhead and there's no shade to be found.

It forces me and Damon to hit up a small, man-made lake like one might find at some crappy summer camp, affectionately called Hepatitis Lake. It's not bad, in spite of its foreboding nickname, brackish green tint and all of the trash floating around in it, and was actually treated for the event. The water isn't as cool as I want, but it still offers a break from the brutal heat. Juggalos bob up and down in the water or dig their feet deep down in the mud outside the shallow-end barricade. Sitting out on the dock are about twenty-five Juggalos and maybe three Juggalettes. Besides the simple age-old act of shoving your buddy in the water when he's not paying attention, they are having a lot of fun fucking around with the balance of the dock. Too many of them stand at one corner of the dock, then the side opposite rises up several feet and a whole passel of flaily-limbed, skinny Juggalos and fat tattooed hairy ones tumble off into the lake, laughing and cursing. There's something endlessly comic about it that keeps me watching and waiting for it to happen.

Thin Juggalos buoy on their big girlfriends, arms wrapped around each other as they make out, then tease and splash other friends in their small group. After years of only knowing the Juggalos from their video blogs, poorly spelled message board postings and angry, defensive retorts to haters via Youtube comments, I'm warmed by the adorableness in these young misfits. Everybody is completely stoked to be out here. For the

Juggalos, this is Shangri-la on earth, a small piece of heaven before returning to lives that are probably at best banal, but more likely oppressive and hard. They laugh! They freestyle! They drink Faygo! They throw shit! It's still morning and the heat already starts to break down me and Damon, but give the Juggalos a bit of shade or a lake and they won't stop the party. They scraped, saved, hustled, borrowed and stole every cent they could to get down here and now they're ready to live it up.

My mind slips back to three weeks ago, drunk as piss and buying the plane ticket online that began my trip to the Gathering. It was a crossing of the Rubicon for me. The Gathering slid right up next to my own festival I attend every year, one I won't name in order to protect it. That same night I packed to head out to the woods for two weeks with my friends. I didn't plan ahead for the Gathering. I knew I was going, but due to my own self-doubt, I put off planning for it until the last minute and came out ill-prepared. I guess, like the Juggalos, I'm a bit of a floob. I fuck things up. I lack confidence and I come from a place where everyone pretty much told me I was bound to fail.

Days after I bought my ticket, all of my friends lay under blankets in a meadow, under a broad belly of stars, miles from any civilization in a Northern California forest, we drop E and huddle together close while the temperature of our bodies drop with the night air. We laugh that night, long into the morning, then watch the sun rise, waking amorous color around us. I refuse to talk of this undertaking of the Gathering to my friends, but I need the support of my people more than anything at this moment.

There's something to be said for completely stripping your guard down—having these moments go on for a few days and a couple weeks are enough to shed the city for a while. We strip ourselves of all outside worries, of all the condescending eyes, all the traffic and debt and newscasts of war and entropy. Hopefully we mentally stay in that place for a good long time; with at least a few days to let our true self emerge from our layers of armor—armor that's so much a part of us we can't remember strapping some of it on. We stop thinking twice about what we say and do and bullshit perceptions. For a few a days we slip out of the judgmental eyes of the world, and spend them laughing and romping and getting fucked up or doing whatever the hell it is we do with our friends, whatever it was that brought us together in the first place. We just feel...home. This is the reason people do seemingly cheesy things like Burning Man Festival or a science fiction con, or whatever it might be for whoever one might be. And sometimes one may grow weary of some of the bullshit elements of the event or the actions of some of the other folks that show up and fuck things up, but the tightness with people that actually "get it," and the feelings of solidarity, leaves an imprint. As humans we need these zones, these islands. Fuck the world!

And the Juggalos probably hate hippies as much as I do.

"BLAM!" An M-80 goes off on the other side of the Hepatitis Lake blowing a hole in the side of someone's tent. Juggalos on the dock start shouting, "YOU FUCKED UP! YOU FUCKED UP!," at the 'lo who set it off. The complete lack of security gives the Gathering a weird *Lord of the Flies* feel. When someone does something that goes against what the majority of Juggalos deem appropriate, the "YOU FUCKED UP" chant will go up. If enough of them are displeased some action takes place. I've heard tell of a thing called a Juggalo jury where a Juggalo will be tried by a court of his or her peers, and if found guilty, they'll receive some form of punishment for their wrongdoing. So, for instance, if a Juggalo stole from another, he doesn't get thrown out of the Gathering by a bunch of security goons, he just serves out his sentence.

This is a good example of the sympathy Juggalos show each other. One of the penances is doing time in Juggalo Jail, a small, round, red and yellow barred structure resembling something that might be on top of some kind of playground equipment. A convicted Juggalo can even watch the acts from their cell, as it's located right in front of the stage. It's all in good fun. Juggalos fuck up sometimes, but they keep each other in check. They also use the "FAM-UH-LY" chant to regulate the Gathering. It gets the 'los to come to their senses; they're all here for Clown Love and the "FAM-UH-LEE" chant reminds them of that. It's used to stop fights and to stop people from representing the Family poorly. This (as of yet) benign ochlocracy keeps the Gathering from utter chaos. There are twenty-thousand people here for God's sake. ICP puts a lot of faith in the Juggalo Family to keep things in order this way; they have a lot banked on it with as many folks are out here.

The first people we make buddies with are Jared and Mark. In the field also acting as a parking lot where we're all camped, we are laughing at some hothead attendant, a hired local who just chewed all three of us out over how we parked and set up camp—nothing like bonding over some random asshole to break the ice between strangers. Jared is a white dude in his mid-thirties from Lansing, Michigan. He wears a T-shirt of a Michigan sports team and shorts. He's here with his stepbrother, Mark, who was also a nice enough fellow, but too stoned out of his gourd to articulate most of the time. It's their first Gathering, too.

"Are you a Juggalo?" I ask Jared.

"Well,' he pauses, 'yeah, I guess," he says, answering with an awkward smile.

I'm not sure why he's reluctant to say he's a Juggalo. Perhaps he doesn't feel like he's down enough to quite take on the title, or if he really doesn't feel like one and feels put on the spot. The question itself, though, is out of the ordinary here and I'm glad, for my own safety, that I posed it to him first. Of course he's a Juggalo—this is the Gathering of the Juggalos.

"Are you?" He asks, going along with how I kicked off the conversation.

"No, I just like rap, and I'm a writer so I figured I'd come out here to check it out," I say.

I continue to use this as my excuse for being out at the Gathering if I chose to out myself, though sometimes I think it best to leave out the "writer" part. After a while, Damon comes over and I introduce him. Jared sits in his car playing hip-hop and rolling blunts while chatting it up with us.

"Yeah,' he turns to me after a while and says, more confidently, 'I'm a Juggalo. I got into them back in '95 with their Ringmaster album. I was a really big fan when they were just coming up, but I wasn't into where they were going with their later stuff. Now I'm going back and catching up on some the stuff I've missed."

He pulls down his sock to show us his right calf where he's tattooed with the Ringmaster logo.

"It's actually backwards,' he says with a smile. 'The tattoo artist fucked up and put the transfer on backwards. I just say you're supposed to look at it in the mirror."

Dark Carnival

It's a full moon and the riddle's are calling/Three more cards and the skies will be falling/But don't take it from me, I'm just a clown/Wicked Clown, wicked town/Juggalugagaluga lick it down
-Insane Clown Posse

Because of my vision, and what happened over the next couple of days, I began to realize that I either was chosen for a grand purpose in this world, or I had gone completely insane.
-Violent J

In the early nineties ICP stood for Inner City Posse, a gangsta rap group made up of Violent J, Shaggy 2 Dope and Shaggy's brother, John Utsler, who performed as John Kickjazz. There was some verisimilitude to their criminal-minded lyrics as they lived like street thugs, except they weren't actually a gang. Nonetheless, their first release, an EP titled *Dog Beats*, became a regional hit and they started getting threats from actual gangs in the Detroit area. They changed their name in order to distance them-selves from their gangsta themes and avoid the beef they were getting. They also felt they should represent Detroit more by not playing the same kind of rap L.A. was exporting at the time with groups like N.W.A. They took some notes from Esham, a Detroit rapper who used Satanic imagery, extreme violence and a macabre horror movie tone in his songs as allegory to illuminate issues those in the ghetto struggled with. With song titles like, "Red Rum" and "Kkkill The Fetus," Esham called his music "acid rap," and strongly influenced what would soon be known as horrorcore (so much that he is often credited with being the inventor of the genre). ICP wanted to get on the horrorcore tip but they wanted to put their own twist on it and thus came up with Wicked Shit. They also wanted to keep the initials ICP so the locals would know they were the same group. At this point Violent J had his epiphany. According to his autobiography, *ICP: Behind The Paint,* it hit him all at once and he knew he figured it out.

"Listen...I got that Detroit shit...our shit is going to have tons of our own humor mixed in, right? CLOWNS! We're scrubby-ass killer clowns. Then it hit me all at once–BOOM! Let's all paint our faces like clowns and be the Insane Clown Posse: clowns who murder and kill people who deserve to be murdered or killed. 'WHOOOOSH!'"

While they were already getting pretty popular without it, the grim imagery made them huge underground stars. The people who "deserved it" included child molesters, wife beaters, racists and "richies," but also included contradictions, including women and animals.

Later, on the night of J's epiphany, the Clown revealed itself even further. Violent J went home "excited as fuck about the whole thing" and while still wide awake he had a vision in which his whole room turned into an eerie carnival.

> "The carnival was completely surrounding me on all sides, and was as twisted and strange as fuck. Standing not ten feet away from me was the Clown I had seen many times in my dreams, but this time he was all too real as he sat staring back at me. He had white clown makeup on in a strange pattern. He wore a pink jester's hat, and a clown suit with big clown shoes and white gloves. He held in his left hand a deck of giant playing cards. Each one was a joker's card, like you might see in a normal deck of cards."

The Clown started dropping the cards on the ground, the whole time talking to him with no words coming out of his mouth. Just before the last card dropped Violent J found himself high above everything and he could see that the carnival was headed to a town. Then blackness...

> "Then loud as fuck. All I could hear was screams and the sounds of chaos and people dying and bizarre laughter. It got mega loud as fuck, but I saw nothing," says Violent J

After he came down from his vision, he says, "I began to realize that either I was chosen for a grand purpose or completely insane." He decided to go with the former and started the Juggalo faith, known as the Dark Carnival. He felt he was called by these "spirit ninjas" to spread the message of the Dark Carnival on earth and to lead people on a pure and a righteous path. The tenets of the Dark Carnival revealed themselves in the next six ICP albums, called the Joker's Cards. Insane Clown Posse albums teach moral lessons where the wicked are judged for their bad actions and sent to Hell's Pit, and those who lived a morally upright life go to Shangri-la, the Juggalo heaven. This is the wisdom they grace upon the Juggalos through all of the gore and violence.

> "The strangest thing that happened to me after that vision was that suddenly ideas and images would pop into my head with ease as if there was an energy or beings who where (sic) channeling through me and feeding me this information. It became all too clear to me what my purpose in life was. For me, the Dark Carnival in my vision is something real and something that is coming. Maybe it won't look exactly like it did in my vision, but something out there is coming, and it is going to consume all those souls who are not pure" writes Violent J.

They believe the violence in their songs "hold up a mirror that might help some people get on a more righteous path, so they won't spend eternity burning in Hell." Yet Violent J also claims not to "believe all the traditional Bible beliefs as to what is considered a sin."

This is where it all gets very confusing. First of all, I can't say I've listened to every album by ICP, but I listened to quite a few of them during my research and the message is lost on me. I have trouble picking up on the morality in the metaphors. The songs just seem to me like a lot of rap about hacking people up and some scatological stupidity about stuff like eating Monopoly and shitting out Connect Four. Sure, I understand the morality in songs about inflicting violence on child molesters, wife beaters, and other "people that deserve it," but those morals contradict with songs about attacking women, bystanders, and other innocents I have trouble believing deserve it. Hell, even a dog and a cat get it in some of their songs.

The only consistency in ICP is the inconsistency. Inconsistencies of thought and hypocrisy pepper everything Insane Clown Posse says. As an outsider, I see inconsistency itself as the Dark Carnival message. As spiritual leaders and prophets, ICP take no account for their lyrics or their actions. They quickly point out only Juggalos understand the lyrics, which creates an easy out for them because most Juggalos are followers of ICP and repeat what Violent J and Shaggy say verbatim with little question. They're even known to physically attack people who criticize ICP. So to understand the Dark Carnival, one must understand ICP, and to understand ICP one must be a Juggalo. It's a Tilt-A-Whirl of thought which makes the Juggalos unable to see the hypocrisies and holes in the Dark Carnival faith and allows ICP to never take responsibility for their actions.

But Violent J takes it a bit further and often says to be a Juggalo, one doesn't have to wear HatchetGear or drink Faygo, and one doesn't even have to like Insane Clown Posse or Psychopathic Records to be a Juggalo. He says some Juggalos haven't even heard of ICP or even know they're Juggalos, but if one is a Juggalo the truth of the Dark Carnival will come to them. However, I've yet to see this happen. Every Juggalo I've met buys into the whole package. Personally, if the truth comes from a guy in face paint swigging a two-liter of generic soda, I'm fucked for believing it. And that's how most people feel. This is why there are no Wicked Shit fans. If you get it, you buy the whole package...and you're a Juggalo. If not, you can't stand it, from the clown makeup to the Wicked Shit; it's all the lowest common denominator of art, and you certainly don't want anything to do with the Family or the Dark Carnival. If Violent J preaches the truth, it certainly is only for a select few. There is no stronger addiction than rightness—it carries with it it's own reward and relieves the believer of the crisis of a question.

Faygo Pop

*We was butt naked all over the floor, it felt weird, though,
'cause we was at the Faygo store*
-Insane Clown Posse

Faygo Soda is a huge thing with the Juggalos. Insane Clown Posse drenches the crowd with it at their shows, throwing and drop-kicking countless two-liter bottles into the audience or spraying it all over them with a fire hose. No raincoats are worn as the crowd joyfully gets drenched in the sugary stickiness, writhing in it as one solid mass. Faygo Soda is a generic pop from the Michigan area and comes in fifty different flavors. As kids, ICP loved drinking it. It was cheap, so they had it around their homes. Their connection to it seems to be out of a combination of regional pride and working class symbolism. They've also always denied any sponsorship from Faygo, claiming it's just a part of the Juggalo mythology.

It's disturbing how much the Juggalos like Faygo. There's a physical association with it, one that might live in the body, after one has made a connection with the Family at an ICP show. Something triggers a memory of the time a Juggalo found "it"—when they finally felt like they came home. And there doesn't seem to be any Juggalos who don't like Faygo. All of them swear by it. It's symbolic to me, not of Clown Love, but of how ICP seems to possess so much sway over the Juggalos' lives, even down to swearing allegiance to a brand of pop.

The origin of Faygo being a big part of the Dark Carnival starts out rather simply. Insane Clown Posse procured a bunch of two-liters of Faygo and set them up on the side of the stage during one of their very first shows. Violent J says they just wanted the audience to be able to see it sitting there because they rapped about it in their songs. During the set some kid flipped J off and he got so pissed he just opened one of the bottles and chucked it at the kid. The kid threw it back and suddenly the crowd grabbed the rest of the bottles and started spraying them everywhere, and the soda has been part of the ICP legend ever since.

At 1:45, in a tent called the Bomb House, Ron Jeremy—the porn star famous for his enormous dong—still hasn't shown up to host the wet T-shirt contest in which a bunch of Juggalettes will be hosed down with Faygo. I showed up twenty minutes late, myself, and am still waiting. A whole lot of restless 'los and, taking into account the entertainment, a significant amount of 'lettes, pack into the circus-sized tent. The mass of what may be up to eight-hundred bodies in the tent kicks the heat inside up to 115 or 120 degrees. A huge circle breaks out in the middle of the crowd and in it is a massive amount of empty beer cans and Faygo bottles which ninjas jump in and grab.

The front half shouts,

"FUCK THE BACK! FUCK THE BACK!"

"FUCK THE FRONT! FUCK THE FRONT!" The rear calls out in response.

And trash just flies and flies. My position in the middle isn't safe, as bottles are winged joyfully in every direction. Bottles, cans, wadded-up paper plates and empty balloons that no longer contain nitrous fly from one side to another. As I try to take some photos of the battle I get pegged in the head with a beer can from behind. I turn to a short, skinny, 'lo with white-boy cornrows about ten yards away and half-hidden in the crowd, he throws up his hands in the universal sign of "I dunno" with a mischievous grin, hamming it up. I flip him the bird with a smile. He appreciates it. Then the crowd moves about and obscures him completely.

Ron Jeremy still hasn't arrived, nor is there any sign of the soon to be wet T-shirted girls. The Juggalos grow weary of trash-fighting, but still they wait. The tent is insufferably hot and the crowd noticeably thins out, but most remain.

Ron Jeremy shows up about 45 minutes late, where he's pelted with trash by the crowd and booed.

"YOU FUCKED UP! YOU FUCKED UP!" the antsy, overheated crowd chants at Jeremy.

Eventually, they settle down enough for Jeremy to drag some 'lettes on the stage to start the Faygo wet T-shirt contest.

About eight barely legal girls start shaking their asses and getting sprayed down with bottles of Faygo from the 'los in the crowd. The T-shirts are pretty much non-existent, and it doesn't take long for the bikini tops to come off as well. Jeremy encourages them to get into some girl-on-girl action. The winner will receive a grip of Psychopathic Records merch and they're working hard for it, but they seem to be having too much fun to be strictly in it for that; these girls love to perform. A couple of the girls on the stage are pretty heavy. Juggalo body/beauty standards differ from mainstream society—a Juggalette is a Juggalette and thus hot for being a Juggalette. Fat girls can get mad respect in the Dark Carnival. They get up and grind the pole with the skinny 'lettes and the 'los are stoked.

Feeling like I've had enough and nauseous from the heat, I work my way to the rear of the tent where I see a shirtless 'lo who looks to be in his late twenties. He sports a tattoo of the Batman logo with the words Twiztid, a Psychopathic Records band, in place of the superheroes name. He kneels down and a child of five or so pours blue Faygo soda over him.

I walk in a heat-induced fog back to the van. I cut through the Midway, past the corn dogs, the elephant ears, the Fat-Ass Chops and Jumbo Bitch Beaters. Sun sick and irritable, I find it hard not to think about how unattractive I find the Juggalos. It goes beyond the fact that I don't understand their fashion or aesthetics. Most of the Juggalos are unhealthy looking—skinny and pale or flabby and obese. I watch them munch elephant ears while lounging in pockets of shade and I find myself judging them harshly, which only results in me feeling uncomfortable with myself. It's the cruelest and easiest thing to pick on someone's physical appearance, but I feel it must be noted. In other subcultures, such as the one that I came up in, punk, it may be easier to be more body positive. Part of the Do-It-Yourself ethic of punk promoted certain health awareness. A husky girl eating greens out of her garden or cooking dumpstered produce is way more acceptable than seeing a whole lot of overweight people eating corn dogs from the midway and swigging generic soda.

It reminds me of my job driving a taxi and working the poorer areas of town, driving folks back from the grocery store and unloading their groceries, everything pre-packaged and all junk food, with few vegetables or fruit. It's becoming clear that the Juggalos, most of them anyway, are oppressed, not because they are Juggalos, but because of their class. They remind me of the folks from the towns I came up in–places I don't want to think about anymore.

"How would my radical West Coast friends act out here?" I wonder. Would they judge everything they see without taking into account why and how it's happening? Probably. What would my feminist friends think of all the entertainment being wet T-shirt contests and oil wrestling and songs about bitches? Offended of course. The Juggalos are judged constantly, but not many gotten down with them to see what they are all about. Then there's me. Me and my self-described pro-sleaze buddy...and whatever I choose to leave out of the tale. But right now I'm just kind of sickened by everything, not to mention heat sick in the sweltering humidity.

I walk past the wide, sprawling Psychopathic Records/HatchetGear merch booth, which provides plenty of shade and items for ICP's working class and struggling "floob" fanbase to purchase. I walk past the autograph tent, which eventually provides shade if one waits long enough to get into the tent by way of the snaking line feeding into the tent. People wait endlessly in the long line in the blazing sun, sweating and skin burning as they wait to get their stuff signed by their favorite Psychopathic Records artists. I wonder how much I could hock Violent J's autobiography for if I get it signed, but the line is very, very long.

Insane Clown Posse constantly boasts about their success, and how the Juggalos aided in that success. Even though they're the "most hated band in the world," they sell tons and tons of CD's, stickers, hats, ball jerseys and shorts, die-cast Hatchetman necklaces and so on, because of the rabid commitment of their followers. ICP often makes different versions of an album so they sell multiple copies. They gloat over the fact they move so many units even though physical media is a dying industry. They take pride in the commitment from their followers. So fuck the mainstream, fuck the music industry, they say. They got theirs.

"They lose thousands of dollars on the Gathering every year. They just do it to give something back to us," Juggalos tell me.

And the Juggalos appreciate this selfless act.

Violent J and Shaggy may tell us how to get to Shangri-la, but as far as how to live until then, well, it looks like we're on our own. The point of Wicked Shit doesn't seem to be encouraging the elevation of their followers. Violent J is no Chuck D, pushing his fans to educate themselves and to rise above. It's clear the highest good of Juggalo culture is to simply be a Juggalo. I say this, not making light of the importance of Clown Love and taking care of their Family, but for a subculture, I notice how Juggalos don't seem empowered by their leaders, who instead encourage them to be floobs. I fail to understand such leadership, but Juggalos aren't unique. I find it all too common in our society, for the more empowered the follower becomes the less power the leader holds. So the Juggalos appreciate the selfless acts of gratitude from ICP, like the Gathering, while ICP remains ennobled and down for the underdog and encouraging the Juggalos to take pride in being floobs…so long as they remain floobs.

But I'm forgetting the Dark Carnival, and how God called on ICP to lead the Juggalos out of Hell's Pit to Shangri-la. Who needs knowledge when someone pimps the Ultimate Truth? Especially while doing it through fresh rap songs?

"You have to respect ICP," is something I hear Juggalos say all the time out here. But as much as I try to see where Juggalos come from on this, I can't respect ICP. Maybe I'm too much of a set-in-my-ways radical, but I'm only able to see them as poverty profiteers and power hungry sociopaths. And this makes me a hater.

Shangri-la and Dark Carnival Defined

The truth is we follow God
We've always been behind Him
the Carnival is God and may all Juggalos find Him...
May the Juggalos find God
We're not sorry that we tricked you
the Carnival will carry on
Suck my nuts, bitch, fuck you...
-Insane Clown Posse

The Love Wagon drives by slowly.

"FUCK YOUR WALKIN'! FUCK YOUR WALKING'!FUCK YOUR WALKIN'!" The Juggalos chant from the wagon.

I grab some of the ever-present trash on the ground and whip it at the young 'los.

"Let's get on!" Damon shouts and starts limp-jogging, his left leg stiff.

We climb on despite the rule we're not supposed to get on when it's moving. Like all the rules at the Gathering, it's just there to be broken. It's mostly a younger group of 'los on the hard wooden wagon and it's complete chaos, except for the unison of their chanting.

The wagon turns a corner passing the Bomb House where a 'lo and his 'lette set up a table with probably around fifty assorted sizes and colors of plastic bottles filled with water, all for the sole purpose of chucking them at the Love Wagon. Damon and I duck and cover our heads as the Love Wagon riders take this barrage like soldiers, the young 'los smiling and flipping-off the offense and throwing back the bottles.

The Love Wagon continues on as the Juggalos chant in unison.

"FUCK YOUR WALKIN'!" they chant to 'los walking.

"FUCK YOUR CAMPIN'!" they chant to 'los camping.

"FUCK YOUR CORN DOG!" they chant to a corn dog.

And...Of course, the wild, primal call of "SHOW YOUR TITS!" when there are...tits.

"THAT SMELLS GOOD! THAT SMELLS GOOD! THAT SMELLS GOOD!" They chant to a grill full of wieners.

"OLD SCHOOL TITTIES! OLD SCHOOL TITTIES! OLD SCHOOL TITTIES!" They chant as we pass a completely naked sixty-year-old displaced hippie and her fully clothed partner.

When we round the curve, the second stage comes into view. A huge flank of 'los and 'lettes emerge from behind a staggered row of tents and bombard us with countless water balloons, the scene comparable to one of those old medieval movies where a phalanx of archers shoot a ton of arrows all at once, blackening the sky. We're getting soaked and laughing hysterically at the Love Wagon's honorable defeat. Then we jump off the Love Wagon and get down to business.

"TITTIES! TITTIES!" We hear as it fades into the distance.

What was the question I was set to ask? Oh yeah...what is Shangri-la? I take out the tape recorder and start asking questions.

"Shangri-la and what it means to me is all about Karma, you know,' a Juggalo named Jason, 21, tells us, 'Violent J...He wanted to show two different after lives and, personally, I really don't believe in an afterlife. But Shangri-la is, like, a paradise where you can be at Hakuna Matata, a good state of mind. No worries. You know, you're just there, kickin' it. You've got Hell's Pit and you've got Shangri-la and you didn't want any of the Juggalos to go to Hell's Pit, 'cause if you listen to the CD's, Shangri-la is all about the Juggalos...all about the Juggalos. And then Hell's Pit's just all dark and evil."

Many Juggalos repeat this "just kickin'" it phrase, or say "just chillin'" when they refer to what Shangri-la means to them. Some of them believe it's something in the future and others, like Jason, believe it's in the present, but they all throw these two phrases around as if they see Shangri-la as a place of respite and peace—a place they can be themselves in a world in which they feel like outcasts.

> "I believe that this world will end. It will be destroyed, taking all the people who aren't followers of the Dark Carnival,' Bloodrain says as he sips on my whiskey bottle, 'then a new world will be made here which will be Shangri-la for Juggalos."

I ask him about good people who aren't Juggalos, if they'll be saved and allowed entry into this post-earth afterlife. I feel he thinks I'm referring to myself, but I'm actually referring to someone more like…his grandma, who I'm assuming isn't a Juggalo. Coming from a Pentecostal background, I know full well the weight having all the truth, knowing their family and friends are headed towards eternal damnation for being non-believers, can have on the believer, and I find this aspect of any faith interesting.

> "Yeah, if they're good people they'll make it, too,' Bloodrain says, and points a thumb to his buddy, 'can he get a drink?"

> "Sure," I say and he passes it.

His painted-up friend takes a humble swig and hands it back to me.

I think the "good people" clause may be what Violent J is saying about how Juggalos exist who don't rock the HatchetGear and have never heard of ICP and even some Juggalos who don't even know they're Juggalos. I've heard several Juggalos repeat this saying; they know Juggalos who have never heard of ICP, and I think what they're getting at is there's some kind of Shangri-la pass for ninjas, like your family and friends who don't willingly participate in the Dark Carnival. Nevertheless, a lot of Juggalos I talk to find Bloodrain's apocalyptic take on Shangri-la controversial. They think he's a little out there and they don't like the implied judgment day. In spite of Violent J's hell and damnation tenets, most Juggalos are more flippant about it all, and shrug off the afterlife aspect of it all together.

"It's a big-ass stepping stone,' Topher, a chubby, warm-hearted Juggalo from Cincinnati says, 'it's just like the dude who said we're all gonna take over the world, blah-di-blah-blah...I really don't think that's what needs to happen, I just think it's a whole mentality of freedom...Once everyone feels like they're free, then they are. You don't feel free, you're not free. That's what freedom's about."

"I don't see it only as an afterlife. This (the Gathering) is Shangri-la because it's the happiest place on earth. This could be Shangri-la. Heaven could be Shangri-la. Whatever keeps 'em out of my face could be Shangri-la." Says Dom from Milwaukee, who defines Shangri-la as "The happiest place on or off earth."

On a sensationalistic level, it's disappointing the Juggalo's Dark Carnival comes across as so simple to them. That, in spite of the Judeo-Christian overtones, Shangri-la means just kicking it with your homies at a place like the Gathering, or "just people taking care of each other, like it should be," as another 'lo told me. But it is heartening that the Dark Carnival and the Juggalo Family stems from a basic human need. To most Juggalos the two are one and the same. They come to this understanding when they see an ICP show or attend the Gathering, and realize their faith and the Family are intertwined.

"We're fuckin' in Shangri-la right now. Juggalo Island all day,' Jame-o from Atlanta tells me. 'This is what I fell into. I fell into something and finally felt like something accepted me. You know what I mean? I can't imagine heaven being much better."

"If you see anybody that's too fucked up, please, get them some water and let them live." he adds.

Insane Clown Posse disappointed a lot of Juggalos when they released the 6th and final Joker's card album. The highly-anticipated album dropped the final message of the Dark Carnival on the song "Thy Unveiling," which starts with the sound of a thunderstorm and builds with a deep and ominous tension listing off the previous five Joker's Cards: Carnival of Carnage, The Ringmaster, The Riddlebox, The Great Milenko, The Amazing Jeckel Brothers, And The Wraith...

> "Looks like we're all out of time, brother,' Violent J says, 'everybody's out of time. Fuck it, we gots to tell em...'"

They go on to tell the Juggalo's "the Dark Carnival is God, not sorry that we tricked you. May the Juggalos find God."

This caused quite a stir amongst the Juggalos. Some of them felt betrayed and fooled into Christianity, many converted, and others adapted their own personal philosophies and spirituality to fit the final message, but from my understanding few Juggalos felt upset enough to up and leave their Family.

Sid, a transgender African-American Juggalo from Ohio, tells me he was raised in a rigid and oppressive Pentecostal family. He sees the Dark Carnival as a way to reconnect with his spirituality without all of the fear and hate that surround his upbringing. It makes things simpler, and he says,

> "Shangri-la to me is, basically...It's like Heaven for people who are good people. You don't have to be a Juggalo to go to Shangri-la, for me it seems like I can just be a good person and do good things and go there. The whole thing that pissed me off about Christianity is, you know, I mean there's Christians who want to go to Shangri-la, obviously, but I'm just saying, how they think about Heaven, it's like you gotta do all this perfect shit. If you're not perfect you're not gonna make it. Like if you don't speak in tongues, if you don't do this, this, this, this and this then you're fuckin' not gonna make it. And it's just like, there are really good people out there who are not in Heaven—to their standards—because they're not speaking a certain language? That doesn't make any sense. So for Shangri-la, you can do, you know, whatever, just be a good fuckin' person, help out people every once in a while or something and you're gonna go up there, you know. Its just another version of Heaven for people who aren't accepted."

Other Juggalos believe the Dark Carnival is the only way and people will spend an eternity in Hell's Pit if they live in ways that aren't moral and righteous, but this morality, based more off simple goodwill, encompasses a wider path than the narrow one of fundamentalist Christianity. Bubbles, a thin, female Juggalo with long dreads and adorned in countless glowsticks and a puffy day-glo dress explains,

> "Shangri-la really is a paradise to me, whenever your day comes, whenever the reaper is knocking on your door, The Wraith has like, as I like to call it, he's gonna set you straight. If you steal, and you hate, and you have prejudice, all those things that cause horrible, horrible things, you will go to Hell's Pit, and you will sit there with the demon and burn forever. And the afterlife, like, if you use your karma and you do your shit straight, you'll end up in Shangi-La. Sippin' on a Faygo and smokin a blunt all day long."

The fluidity of each Juggalo's interpretation of the Joker's Cards interests me. Unlike Christianity, it appears every Juggalo respects his fellow 'los take on the Cards. No one claims a monopoly on spiritual truth, and even though some of them, like Bubbles, might literally believe in Hell's Pit, they don't come across as high 'n' mighty enough to tell anyone they're going there. Instead, they look at the Six Cards as warnings against immoral action in their own lives. Unlike the Christian beliefs the Dark Carnival is rooted in, it's up to the individual 'lo to work out their own salvation. How a 'lo chooses to view the Cards is respected as the truth for them. Juggalos don't argue each other's personal doctrine.

Maybe this harkens back to what Violent J says about how some Juggalos don't even know they're Juggalos. And while the Juggalos have many words for a fake Juggalo (a juffalo or a juggahoe), they generally don't damn the non-Juggalos. Not to say that Juggalos don't harbor some resentment for the rest of the world, at times, but it seems to be based more around defensiveness than spiritual elitism.

> "They gave us some shit for it, but whatever, I like it," Neil from Massachusetts says to me when asked about the "Miracles" video.

Neil is one of the rare Juggalos I speak to who even knows how big the level mockery of the "Miracles" video reached. Most Juggalos I meet who are aware of the mocking are pretty flippant about it, though some can get pretty defensive. Juggalos are used to getting crap for following the "most hated band in the world" and don't expect those outside of the Dark Carnival to understand.

"I love the 'Miracles' video,' a Juggalo named Fuckstick relays, 'their message is they're trying to get to everybody (to have), like, pretty much, peace, love and harmony. They want everything to work, their song is about that message. So with 'Miracles' they quit hiding the message, OK. All their older stuff they hid the message and a lot of people didn't get it. 'Miracles'...it's out there. It's like a slap in the face, you get the message. It's about the world. Everything's beautiful. They're not really saying screw science or anything. Scientists just are oblivious and, well, not all scientists, but some of them are pretty cool about it but a lot of scientists are oblivious and naive to the fact that miracles exist. They want fact for everything and there isn't fact for everything."

Fuckstick proceeds to tells me that even when ICP sing songs about more insidious things, the point is to push the message of peace and love.

"Even the shit talking about killing, they're not really talking about going out and killing someone. They're rapping from someone else's perspective," he says.

The duality of Wicked Shit (violent and mean-spirited lyrics promoting faith and love) confuses the outsider. When I tried to put myself in the mind of the Juggalo to figure it out, it only resulted in cognitive dissonance. Talking to them doesn't make it any clearer, but it illuminates why the Family doesn't have the same struggle with it. The very fact any messages of love and faith are obtuse and untenable make it easy for Juggalos to piece the messages into something they are able grasp. Add the Clown Love the Juggalos receive from the Family and it's hard for them to dismiss any sacred or spiritual messages in the Dark Carnival. Somehow, they make it work, but it's hard for the outsider to understand perhaps because they go through the back door on a lot of things. Through objectification the Juggalos learn to appreciate different body types, through materialism they find sacrament, through violence they discover love, and through don't-give-a-fuck-nihilism they find faith. I think those notions explains why so many Juggalos told me if I really wanted to know about the Dark Carnival or Shangri-la I needed to ask every Juggalo, because it differs for everyone. Juggalos, however, don't ask anyone—the answers are in the Joker's Cards.

Four Cornerstones of Juggalo Attraction

We'll never die alone,
Juggalos will carry on,
Swing our hatchets if we must,
Each and every one of us...
-Insane Clown Posse

Damon and I catch a few acts on the main stage but mostly we just drink and run around. We manage to see Blaze Ya Dead Homie on the main stage with about 15,000 Juggalos. Blaze's whole shtick is he's an ex-gangsta rapper who was killed and rose from the dead as a Juggalo to rap Wicked Shit. I smile and think of how that's an interesting metaphor for a lot of fallen off old school rappers who jumped on the Juggalo bandwagon into an immediate captive fan base. Vanilla Ice received a great amount of respect from the 'los. Ice-T hosted a documentary about the Gathering called *ICP: A Family Underground* and ICP features him on a few songs. Most notoriously, Coolio went as far as getting a Juggalo tattoo and spelled "Juggalo" wrong.

For the record, Blaze, like a lot of acts we've seen out here, puts on a good show. While I'm not entirely sure I'd see him in a different context, he deserves props. Next, Twiztid, tonight's headliner, performs. I'm curious to see them as they're second only to ICP in the Psychopathic Records Family.

Jamie Madrox, a fat white guy and Monoxide Child, a skinnier white guy, compromise Twiztid, and together they rap about sex, violence and alienation in a juvenile way with a lot of Gothic imagery. To distinguish themselves from ICP, they paint their faces completely white and wear eye contacts which give them beady black and menacing pupils. They keep their hair short with little braids on top, a style they made popular among the Juggalos.

We watch them play a few songs, less than half a set, and they bless the audience by allowing them to hear their latest album before anyone else... and walk off the stage. A whole lot of Juggalos wander off into the night, but the amount of Juggalos who stay and face a dark stage listening to the CD over the PA shocks me. A few fluorescent wands and glowsticks light up the night and the soft light of the Midway barely cuts through, but it's really, really dark as the Juggalos listen to a CD of their heroes...the ones they came thousands of miles to see, making it one of the strangest things I've ever witnessed.

As it gets darker, I lose Damon. He goes back to the van to crash out because his gout got to him. I head to the Drug Bridge because, from my understanding, it's a good place to mingle. I'm done taping for the night and quite a bit more drunk. I sit on the rail of the bridge and I'm happy to just observe in my buzzy state. A young 'lo named Kentucky breaks my spell and everything changes.

"Hey, ninja! Are you actually from Kentucky or are you just wearing the T-shirt?" He asks me about my deliberately nondescript T-shirt.

"Huh, what, oh, yeah I'm from Kentucky," I say, not ready to break down where I live now or everywhere else I've lived in my life, and besides, I've spent plenty of time in Kentucky.

"Cool, I just wanted to ask you because they call me Kentucky, but I'm not from Kentucky. That's just what people call me."

He thrusts his hand and shakes mine. We start talking. He hails from somewhere in Illinois, a town I've not heard of. He rocks a thick goatee about six inches long and an oversized Twiztid T-shirt hangs loosely over his thin frame. He's ecstatic to be out here with his Family. And he's all ready to meet more Family (ironically, because that's how he meets me).

"Yeah, I'm not really a Juggalo, I just came out here with my buddy because we like rap and we thought we'd check it out," I tell him.

"Fuck yeah, that's awesome,' he replies, 'it's fucking cool that you came out here and checked it out, man. What do you think of it so far?"

"I think it's pretty awesome. I really like what you have going on."

At this point I feel like I say this truthfully. I don't like everything I see, but I'm starting to appreciate the Family.

"Awesome,' he says. 'So who do you like? I mean you know ICP, right?"

"Yeah,' I say, 'I know some of their stuff and like it. But, hell, I've been seeing Juggalos around my town and I thought I'd come out and see what you're all about. Hell, why not, right, I mean there's some good rap here."

"Man, that's cool. I'm glad you did. I like to put it this way: we're just like hippies except that we dress this way and we have our own thing going on. We're a family and we take care of each other. See that guy over there,' he says pointing out a young, long-haired, guy in tie-dye shirt, 'that's Sam, he's a hippie but he came out with us. He's our buddy, but he goes to festivals and sells shit, you know. But he's cool here. Nobody fucks with you here, man. I mean there's some real douche bag Juggalos out here but most of us just want to show Clown Love. I mean out there we aren't free. Here we're free."

"Are you really free here? I mean, sure, you can buy and do drugs out here, but are you free?"

"Well, there's a loophole here that let's us get away with this,' he says, referring to the fact cops aren't allowed to come on the property because it's private, 'but no, we're even not really free here. But this is where we feel free to just be together with our Family and to be ourselves, away from the bullshit. And that's what it's about, Clown Love. Now I know a lot of the lyrics are really violent, but that's just how we get our aggression out. Sometimes things are so fucked up that I feel like I want to kill somebody. You know? This music's good for getting that out, but really we just want to show Clown Love and take care of each other like a family."

We talk for a long time. I tell him that I came up in punk rock and got involved in punk for some of the same reasons.

"My older brother was punk,' he says, 'He taught me all about it. I think that shits cool."

"But you found your own thing."

"Yeah."

He laughs at my beer, a tall can of shwill called Beer Thirty with the slogan "it's Beer Thirty somewhere" imprinted on the can.

"Ninja, we've been seeing those cans laying all over the place around here and we thought it was hilarious. Beer thirty!"

"Yeah, this shit is all we have to drink, we found a bunch of it on closeout,' I hold the can out in front of him, 'here, man, try it."

Kentucky takes a drink,

"Yeah, ninja, it's not that bad...I guess."

"Not when put up against other shit our broke asses have gotten drunk on."

"No shit, right?' he says and laughs loudly, 'Dude you're awesome! I'm so glad I came up and asked you about your shirt, man. I'm going to tell everyone about you, man. I'm so glad you're here." he says emphatically as he turns to leave.

"Don't do that. I'll get my ass kicked for being a Juffalo!" I shout back.

"Man, you ain't no Juffalo, you're just an old punk rocker."

He turns a few yards off and yells back, waving off my self-deprecation.

I remember Kentucky long after I leave, and I feel I will betray him when I start writing about all of this. He's just a good guy. He doesn't want me to get down with the Clown, he just wants me to respect his people and where they come from. It's the first time I realize how much I will betray these folks who were kind to me and respected me. I will criticize their leaders, and it doesn't matter what I say in favor of the Family, because being critical of Violent J and Shaggy will probably be seen as a betrayal, whether or not it's my intention.

I wanted to understand the appeal and why someone would become a Juggalo. I wanted to confirm a lot of my own suspicions. I hope I have my eyes open and I'm not just seeing what I want, but so far, my experiences at the Gathering seem to back up my theories. I came up with *The Four Cornerstones of Juggalo Attraction*, starting with some initial draws and ending on what keeps one swinging their hatchet for life.

The Four Cornerstones of Juggalo Attraction are the Wicked Clown face, to be reviled, the Family, and the Dark Carnival.

1. **The Wicked Clown face.** A young person who falls outside the cruel standards of high school because they are too nerdy, too socially awkward or maybe even too sociopathic may become an outcast. Physically, they may be too fat, too ugly, or too small. Maybe they are too poor and wore raggedy clothes like Violent J Maybe it all goes back to their home life. Maybe they were beaten or diddled senseless at a young age until their self-esteem shattered so much they didn't stand a chance at fitting in with the popular, or even the unpopular, kids at school. They were floobs and scrubs and their life is a living hell.

    The floob sees an evil clown grinning from a T-shirt and they may go home and look up the name of the band on the shirt. Or maybe the guy wearing the T-shirt takes them in, sends them home with some burnt CD's of Insane Clown Posse and Twiztid. The floob gets it. The music serves as a vessel for their anger, the extreme violence an outlet for all the times they were picked on and unable to defend themselves. The Clown attracts them because the Clown doesn't give a fuck. The Clown is marginalized because it's violent, psychopathic, and insane. The misfit starts to see themselves in the Clown's face. They join the Juggalo Family, embody that evil clown face, and their marginalization becomes voluntary. They portray themselves as violent, wicked, and they'll split your wig if you fuck with them. Don't fuck with a Juggalo.

2. **To be reviled.** Identifying as a Juggalo means shedding an involuntary marginalization for a marginalization of choice. The Juggalo gets tight with their Family and revels in the outcast status. They feel they are involved in something so dark, violent and edgy that the rest of the world simply never understands. They love the hatred they receive from those outside the Dark Carnival. They see through evil clown eyes now. It doesn't matter that most haters of Wicked Shit judge it on unintelligent and violent lyrics or crass merchandising, or perhaps aren't buying the spiritual message, think painting faces up is kind of goofy, and don't care to be covered in soda pop. Maybe haters call ICP's music misogynistic or wish to further deconstruct it. But the Juggalo still feels the haters don't get the music or the Family because everything is just too violent and malevolent, and the world will never understand the obscured positive message behind it all. The Juggalo only becomes more headstrong through this hate, swinging the hatchet because they must.

3. **The Family.** The Family offers important security and Juggalos the community they seek. Welcomed into an elite group of outcasts, they obtain a family of people who really understand them, unlike the abusive one at home. They no longer roam the hallways in their high schools alone, getting their asses kicked. Now they twist their fingers up in the shape of the Wicked Clown symbol and shout "WHOOP! WHOOP!" with all their fellow 'los. They will never die alone. Juggalos will carry on. They're close to the Juggalos in their town but they also know 'los all over the country have their back. The Family is warm, treats them well and accepts them for who they are. The Family is strong and takes care of their own. The Juggalo feels Clown Love and never wants to leave.

4. **The Dark Carnival.** The Dark Carnival seals the deal. The rest of the world doesn't comprehend the Juggalo's faith, just as they don't understand anything about the Juggalo—only the Juggalos understand. The trickiness of how the Dark Carnival faith works confuses and eludes me as always, but why it works is starting to make sense.

One thing to take into account is how Violent J comes across as mentally-ill. Besides the fact he based his entire career on an incident of hallucinating clowns in his living room, he also says he experiences panic attacks where he hears demons speaking to him and telling him he's going to hell. He's known to be highly medicated, depressed and prone to nervous breakdowns. And considering his violent and traumatic background, it's hard to blame him. Nonetheless, everything that makes the Juggalos think Violent J is onto something and getting visions from God would strike a layman as the ramblings of a delusional man. His religious fervor reminds me a lot of the psychology of geniuses such as Van Gogh and Dostoyevsky, who were prone to anxiety, manias, religious revelation and psychotic breakdowns. Any kook who sees weird shit that isn't there could attempt to start a religion, though usually they wander the streets mumbling to themselves or shouting their gospel to nonplussed and disinterested passers-by. Thus, the genius of ICP—they believe in something absurd and kooky but as masters of self-promotion and can easily package and sell it. They know how to trigger their audience and with expert precision they sell it to them. When I first began research, I flipped back and forth between thinking they really believed in their Dark Carnival or were just having us on. In the end it seems like at bit of both. Just like they manipulate the Juggalos, it seems they fool themselves as well. As much as they encourage ignorant floobiness as a way of life for their followers, they have to endorse it themselves. For the non-Juggalo who looks in on the Dark Carnival or watches the "Miracles" video, there's a whole lot of evidence ICP is just plain stupid. But maybe it's not a matter of how intelligent you are, but how you are intelligent.

To achieve this kind of success it's obvious Violent J and Shaggy are charismatic leaders, but would they be without the evil clown makeup? Would they just seem like raving lunatics with wack rhymes and bad tattoos to would-be Juggalos if God hadn't given Violent J the Wicked Clown and the Dark Carnival?

The contradictory nature of Psychopathic Records and Wicked Shit is a slippery, confused (and confusing) reality, to say the least, but simply works because it's always adaptable. Violent J feels called to teach God's message, but he doesn't necessarily believe in the bibles definition of sin. Without the gospel, ICP takes the "righteousness" in scripture and strips it of all accountability. With no solid guidelines for behavior, the Dark Carnival adapts to the lifestyle of the follower. And while it may be easy to go the route of suspecting ICP are having us on with all of this, upon deeper inspection, it doesn't seem to be the case. Instead, ICP created a religion, not unlike a long line of religious zealots, that justifies all their behavior (if they just tweak it here and there). For instance, for all of the justified hatred of "richies" in their songs and culture, Violent J and Shaggy will never be held accountable for their own wealth, nor for gaining it by exploiting their disenfranchised followers. Psychopathic Records, indeed.

So the Dark Carnival is the final hook. A lot of Juggalos I talk to don't trust mainstream religion, some even feel harmed by it. But a more adaptable religion just may be something to help them get through life, especially if it comes with the Wicked packaging. Once they're "down with the Clown," tight with their homies and proudly withdrawn from society, they become receptive to the Dark Carnival's message.

Anti-Intellectualism

*How many times did I walk in and just sit? And have to listen, and learn
all this bullshit/Learnin' history and science, fuckin' wait/Knowin' that, will
that put food on my plate?*
-Insane Clown Posse

After this Gathering, Insane Clown Posse appear on a talk show called
'Attack of the Show.' The show's host asks Violent J and Shaggy what they
do at the end of the day after they take off all of the makeup. "Is [sic]
there geopolitical discussions?"

> "I don't even know what geopolitical means," Violent J, in grinning
> face paint, replies with unsettling delight.

He disturbingly announces this with what seems to be a certain degree of
pride, as if it's cool or noble to be this naive. This is why everyone yucks
it up over the "Miracles" video. It's not the fact the video is spiritual,
despite what ICP claims. (Violent J has made comments, saying, if Bob
Dylan wrote a song like "Miracles" critics would rave about it. However,
Dylan's fundamentalist period was his most unpopular era.) No, the reason everyone makes a joke of the song is because Shaggy 2 Dope thinks
scientists lie to him, which pisses him off. They seem to harbor a vigor-
ous desire to remain ignorant musically and to keep the Juggalos ignorant. While I respect them for their areas of expertise–self-promotion and
creating controversy constructive to building their empire–their message
carries a very strong sense of anti-intellectualism.

> "Stupid people can get more accomplished, because smart people will
> talk themselves out of it," is Damon's take on ICP's success.

It's hard to argue that when hearing songs of theirs like "Stuck Her With
My Wang" where they sing about gluing a woman's titties to the roof
with Elmer's Glue. Violent J and Shaggy really push the floob pride agen-
da, but not as a means to a better end. In his autobiography, Violent J
raves about how he didn't give a fuck about school or his studies, how
he fucked off and wasted those years and it all paid off because he and

Shaggy made millions as rapping clowns. But what does this leave for the Juggalos? He just encourages 'los to follow the Dark Carnival.

As much as ICP talks about how they love their followers, it's essential they remain just that–followers. In a section of the book where J discusses how much they hated and abused groupies because groupies weren't after anything but a piece of their wealth and fame, he makes a disclaimer that he isn't referring to all women, and certainly not Juggalettes. He exclaims he "can most readily relate to the Juggalettes," which may easily translate to "I only relate women who talk about me." It's good of Violent J to not hate all women, but the balance of power is a bit off here, the level of arrogance shocking, but not unheard of. Some of this goes back to the Judeo-Christian beliefs on which the Dark Carnival is based. ICP really treads the line, but they never come right out and say "we're Christian." However, perhaps they might as well after revealing the Dark Carnival is God gracing them a with way to bring The Bible up to date for a new age. As a result, the Dark Carnival falls into the same trappings as its Judeo-Christian predecessors. Believing more in the afterlife than the present one, why shouldn't a Juggalo say "fuck the world?" But could it be more consciously sinister? With ICP pushing teeth-rotting soda, mind-rotting wrestling and puerile horrorcore rap on their followers, instead of education, self-betterment or resistance, as well as floob pride and the promise of Shangri-la, the Juggalos are kept pretty damn busy. Perhaps too busy to question their reverence.

I'm a self-educated, self-published D.I.Y. ex-punk kid, exposed to a much broader underground culture after being empowered by the intellectual side of punk rock. There are two main routes a punk kid can take. One of the many opportunities presented to me was drinking forty-ounces of malt liquor, slamming dope, sitting in the street bumming for change all day, and listening to The Exploited. But on the flip side of that coin lives the intellectual side of punk—the side which resists the establishment, the state, and following leaders and encouraging self-ascension. From there one can go anywhere. It's this side of punk (and all alternative culture) that encourages young people exposed to it to better themselves. As conscious rapper KRS-One said, "knowledge rules supreme."

When Violent J describes his "long goodbye to the Ferndale educational system," in his autobiography, he writes, "motherfuckin' fuck school. I'm 31 years old, today, screamin' fuck school. It wasn't for me after eighth grade." And it wasn't. School is an oppressive place for a lot of kids, especially the poor and working class. Poorly-paid teachers and administration in inner-city schools often target youth who come from bad homes because they act out or just don't know how to act. These teachers may resent their jobs and their place in life and decide to take it out on the kids, trying to drag them down with them. Violent J describes a day when he basically just spaced out, got up during class and starting chucking volumes of an Encyclopedia out the window. His teacher pulled him to the front of the class and tore him down in front of everybody.

> "This kid right here is gonna amount to nothing, You're never going to do anything, Mr. Bruce, are you? You'll come to school your whole life, and you'll never do anything here, will you? You know that? I'll bet that, don't you, Mr. Bruce? Everybody look at this kid. This is Joe. He is happy with himself even though he is gonna mean nothing at all to the world. He will be a nothing. He will never be anything in the world." Violent J recounts his teacher saying way back then.

> "To me,' Violent J writes, 'I was the freshest kid there. I loved that fresh moment in the spotlight. I loved that fresh moment when he said my whole life will be as worthless as a grain of salt. I loved ALWAYS being the underdog. It was my whole motto as a true floob, a scrub, a Juggal-. Not yet."

The Juggalos I talk to love these stories, but few hold success stories of their own. They have trouble making even common conversation without bringing Violent J or Shaggy into it. They live vicariously through ICP's underdog story and through consumerism, crudely attempting to insert themselves into that success story. But the rapping clown is a tapped market, and though a whole lot of Juggalos may put on the makeup and rap evil threats to haters, I doubt they're going to make out like ICP. But I don't think ICP cares about this. Perhaps Insane Clown Posse was an idea that's time had come; perhaps they're true underdogs who saved themselves from poverty. And there is pride in making ones own trails after being rejected, to making ones self a success by ones own rules. And sure, Violent J shouldn't have stuck around in school if it was that hellish for him. But even if Violent J managed to find a way around it, an education or an elevation of the mind is almost always necessary to rise above. Just because he's come this far by rapping about "getting butt-naked and walking through the streets winking at the freaks with a 2-liter stuck in his butt cheeks," doesn't mean the Juggalos can reach this level of success (ironically, he relays this sentiment in the song, "What is a Juggalo?"). I'm not saying Violent J should study geopolitics if big words offend him (hell, I know what geopolitics means, but I still have trouble making rent), nor should Shaggy 2 Dope look up magnets on Wikipedia if he doesn't care to know how they work. It's worked for them so far. However, their followers who look up to them may not get to slide by in life on greasepaint and religious epiphany. To encourage stupidity on the people who look up to them seems irresponsible and exploitative, and doing so while selling them HatchetGear and multiple editions of the same album with limited edition tracks makes it even more insidious, especially when I see the Juggalos hawk them for gas in order to get home from the Gathering. But making such accusations denies Violent J of his prophecy and ICP of their Dark Carnival calling. Nonetheless, they only encourage Juggalos to be Juggalos, not Juggalo lawyers or doctors, not Juggalo grassroots organizers, Juggalo feminists or working class Juggalo defenders or even literate Juggalos. They just sloppily paint "ICP", because Juggalos aren't even encouraged to do graffiti and gets their names up. For a Juggalo to better him or herself, it almost seems they must leave it all behind: the Juggalo Family, the wickedness, the Dark Carnival, and even Shangri-la. That's quite a bit to ask.

If a Juggalo were to care about geopolitics in spite of Violent J's lack of interest in it, would they continue to be a Juggalo? Would anyone listen to them with that clown paint on?

I'm watching the Neden Game in the Bomb Tent. "Neden" in Juggalo slang means pussy, and I'm basically watching a version of that old TV show the Bachelor Game. A tarp separates three male contestants on one side of the stage, and on the other side an empty chair waiting to be filled by a female contestant. Ron Jeremy, decked out in a Hawaiian shirt, hosts the event.

"We need a Juggalette." He says, and a bunch of hands go up amidst shouts of "WHOOP! WHOOP!"

Jeremy's assistant, a mustached, middle-aged, stage hand goes into the audience and comes back with a large...no, a very large contestant. She wears her tank top pulled up and around the back of her neck, exposing a huge belly and long pendulous breasts. He sits her down in the metal folding chair on the other side of the tarp, hidden from the Juggalos to start the game.

Jeremy shakes his head.

> "You're an asshole," he says, likely upset the stage hand picked what he may consider to be an unattractive contestant, probably on the merits of her being topless.

He looks down, still shaking his head, then with a bewildered look, asks the contestant a little bit about herself.

She tells us all where she's from and what she does and then announces she's married,

> "My husband's out there,' she says pointing to the audience, 'he's OK with this."

> "You're an asshole," Ron Jeremy turns and says again to the assistant.

The assistant looks sheepish but says nothing.

> "I need a question from the audience," he says and points out to someone in the audience.

> "Ask them what their job is."

> "I'm in construction," Contestant 1 says.

> "I'm self-employed," Contestant 2 answers with a wink. The crowd taunts him playfully.

"Yeah, right," Ron Jeremy says skeptically.

"I work in a kitchen," the last contestant says.

The questions are kind of basic, and when asked how they make love, one of them tries to pull some nasty, wicked sex shit. Contestant 2 says he likes to take it slow and easy when pleasing a woman.

"I'm going to have to go with what Contestant 2 said" says Contestant 3 creatively.

I can't stop staring at the back of a bright, blue-aired head in front of me. It belongs to a child that couldn't be more than eleven, arms crossed and leaning against the stage watching the game. Somebody suggests a Dance-Off rated by the WHOOP! WHOOP!ing of the crowd, and contestant number three wins.

"Another question from the audience," Ron Jeremy says.

The blue-haired child raises his hand. Ron Jeremy notices him and holds the mic out to him so he can propose a question to the topless woman.

"Ask them if they like fat chicks," he says.

"I can do with a little cushion in my pushin'," Contestant 1 says.

"I can appreciate some big girl love," Contestant 2 says.

"Me too, it's all good," the last contestant says.

When all the questions are done and it comes down to making a decision, the female contestant chooses Contestant Number 3. The two come from around the tarp and meet. Any shock at her size has been dulled by the kid's question or possibly didn't matter, anyway. The winner walks off the stage with his married date, escorting her to a helicopter ride.

"WHOOP! WHOOP!," goes the crowd.

"You're an asshole," Ron Jeremy says to his assistant one more time.

The Wicked Clown Face and the Rebel Flag

Teachin kids what pops taught you
And he's a funky ass bigot too
Fell short of the due respect
Don't speak when I slap ya in your red neck
Fuck all that bullshit you stuck on
Get back on your mule and get the fuck on
Don't look back or I'ma hit ya
Take that red neck bitch out with ya
Spit on your Rebel rag, so fuck you and your Rebel flag!
-Insane Clown Posse

We be the all doing, the all seeing, the all knowing
Chainsaw, baseball bat, and axe toting
Eastside, white trash with tattoos
This is how the fuck we live
This is what the fuck we do
-Twiztid

I don't give a fuck!
-white trash saying

Insane Clown Posse's song, "Rebel Flag," is a reactionary, murderous call-out to racist rednecks, particularly those in the South, the chorus simply repeating "fuck your rebel flag" over and over. The rest of the lyrics consist of line after line of violent threats to white trash bigots.

While racist rednecks may be a worthy target of violence (especially since, towards the end of the song, they single out skinheads and the Klan), that isn't what I find interesting about the song. Nor is it the hypocrisy of militantly anti-bigot groups who are completely oblivious of their own bigotry towards women and those in queer communities. I take these things into consideration, but what I find more interesting is their fixation on the symbol of their targets—the Confederate flag. There are many parallels between the rebel flag and the evil clown face, all having to do with the personal meaning individuals project onto these symbols.

Listening to the song clarifies ICP defines a "redneck" as a racist white guy who lives in the rural South. But the term itself, as most know it, belongs less to a specific region and applies to poor, white, uneducated people anywhere in the States. So, if ICP place their rednecks north of the Mason-Dixon Line, they may find quite a few poor, white folks who also identify with the Confederate Flag, just like they may find a lot of Juggalos in the South who identify with the Wicked Clown face.

I spent most of my teenage years in various small redneck towns in Indiana. One was at the edge of the Gary, Indiana sprawl, another about fifteen miles from the Kentucky border. In those towns I'd see confused white folks driving around with rebel flags waving from their pickups. Sometimes I'd see some mulleted dudes with the flag tattooed on their arms. In the South, there's the whole "heritage not hate" thing, which some may call culturally insensitive, but at least the argument's geographically sound. But when the Rebel Flag flies in a Union state, it doesn't even carry that context. So why would a Northerner take on this symbol?

The easiest dismissal would be to say these Northerners are racist, and I'm sure some of them are. The fact of the matter is, none of the flag wavers I've ever met, specifically, waved the flag as a proclamation of their white supremacy. They wave the Confederate flag to make them feel like rebels, like badasses. For the most part they get behind the flag as a symbol. In an environment with little culture, history, or even a sense of self, the flag serves as just that–a symbol. One to which one applies their own meaning, even if all that meaning portrays is "I don't give a fuck!" It's a subconscious acknowledgment of the way the rest of the world sees them, and in spite of where they live, they will always be seen as rednecks and hicks because of their economic standing.

Where I come from, people didn't stop at the Confederate flag. They also wear the logos of their preferred brand of cigarettes, Camel or Marlboro, on T-shirts and jackets, which they acquire by saving coupons from the sides of the packs. They pride themselves in driving either a Ford or a Chevy, listening Metallica or Guns 'n' Roses, or drinking Budweiser or Miller. But unlike the South, poor white folks in Indiana do not possess as much of a culture to speak of. They don't have the roots, or the family, or regional heritage of the South. There was never much wealth or proud lineage or connection to land or farming to speak of. On the other hand, the South's distinct culture is taken seriously. They pass on strong family traditions, such as Bluegrass music, miner's strikes or Southern Cooking. In Indiana, they were landless, with not much passed on but abuse, debt, and alcoholism, which morphed into crystal meth addiction. Churches don't even stand a chance of saving the "redneck" living in the North. God gets dismissed because families don't have a tradition of going to church. Folks reside in a sort of void with little community, history, traditions or anything to tie them to a sense of pride or place.

While I witnessed all these things in Indiana, I also see these attitudes and desperation starting to spread throughout the country as families lose their traditions by adapting to the Information Age, and their alienation continues with the fall of industry–the death of the "family farm," unemployment, and generations of folks who grew up on television passing their habits on to their children. But then again, maybe it was never a regional thing and it's the same all over the country. Maybe the poor-but-proud, live-off-the-land, rural hick represents just another All-American, rugged individualist archetype. Nonetheless, these folks are losing their traditions, their stories and their histories. Thus, they lose their identities, and as a result they start falling apart. In their fall they grasp onto anything, one of those things being the Confederate Flag.

I'm not calling for a National White Trash history month or a pseudo-racist way of pushing white pride by glorifying or apologizing for poor white folks; nor do I argue we attempt to excuse this group for identifying with a symbol so often associated with slavery. I'm just saying that people apply some sense of self in the Confederate flag, however that might be and however they might choose to explain it.

But back to the Juggalos. The Wicked Clown face works exactly the same way. It comes from the same place, the same sense of disenfranchisement. The disenfranchised white folks who don the Clown face are the same type of people who may fly the rebel flag, except, instead of being proud rednecks, they proudly call themselves Juggalos. They apply the same affiliation to being Wicked Clowns that "rednecks" apply to being rebels. They get a rise out of how the garish and dark aesthetics of the Clown alienate them from the rest of society, and these same folks who may be called hicks, trailer trash and rednecks by the rest of society now identify as proud Juggalos. They grow stronger by any attacks they incur because they have the Family to turn to.

The weight of both symbols also plays a part of their attraction. A Rebel Flag-waving hick fully realizes the controversial nature of such a symbol and history behind it. He partly bases his attraction to it around that, whether it links in some convoluted way to his heritage, or just loudly declares "I don't give a fuck" and acts as a symbol of his rebellion in the most literal of definitions. He bases his attraction, even if not on a conscious level, on the revulsion of others.

To be a Juggalo is to be a target of ridicule from everyone. No matter what subculture one involves themselves in—punk, metal, hippie—one is always better off than a Juggalo. Nobody but a Juggalo respects wearing evil clown makeup on any day but Halloween, nor can anyone but a Juggalo understand the depth of the song "Bugz On My Nutz." The Juggalo aesthetic repulses everyone who isn't a Juggalo. Even punks who appreciate someone like G.G. Allin, who would take Ex-Lax and then throw shit on his audience, are put off by Juggalo culture. Someone cast out by society who becomes a Juggalo is attracted to the subculture by the fact that everyone else hates it and by feeding on negative attention they ultimately win.

I argue the Wicked Clown face for the Juggalo comes from the exact same drive that makes the redneck claim the rebel flag as their symbol. They represent symbols of empowerment for a group of people who have nothing else and status for people who've never had status.

There comes a point when someone is done arguing they aren't white trash or poor or stupid because of where they come from, or the way they talk or the way they let it all hang out and they start wearing the things they are ridiculed for like a badge of honor.

Hepatitis Lake

*Charlie Brown, please, don't come around
Because your weed is doodoo brown
and it smells like the ground
- ABK (Anybody Killa)*

"FUCK THE BEACH! FUCK THE BEACH!" The ninjas on the dock chant to those on the beach.

"FUCK THE DOCK! FUCK THE DOCK!" The ninjas on the beach chant to those on the dock.

The chants continue as the two sides do battle. Barrages of plastic bottles fly back and forth. This battle never ends, renewed by a revolving door of Juggalos who take up sides on whichever one they're closest too. We've spent a long time on the beach getting in and out of Lake Hepatitis to cool off and the fight never ceases. Some of the simpler Juggalos chant and throw shit for up to three hours.

"You got a stupid hat!" a skinny 'lo floating near the beach yells at a fat, shirtless, hairy guy on the dock wearing an enormous straw hat, and throws a bottle at him.

I start laughing out loud at this and Damon turns to me, smiles his canine smile, and repeats the line and it's another moment that I'm glad to share with my best friend.

Our levity catches the attention of a Latino ninja from Florida, who walks over to us.

"Can I film you guys and ask you a question?" he asks.

"Sure." Damon says and I nod to him.

"What do you guys think of the Gathering so far" he asks looking through the lens of a small digital camera.

Damon and I tell him we're having a great time.

> "Did you get any hoes?" He asks. I look away. Damon, closer to him, does the talking.

> "Well, it seems all the cute ones got boyfriends and the rest...aren't so hot..."

Richie puts his phone camera to his side and says,

> "Yeah, Juggalettes aren't known for being very hot." He pauses, "I'm Richie," he introduces himself and shakes our hands.

Richie just arrived today and has spent his time wandering around asking this question, saying he's going to post the results as a film on Youtube when he gets home. We tell him it's awesome to be out here. After chatting for a few more minutes, he tells us to hold on, runs a few yards off and comes back with a collapsible camp chair like Damon's. He sets it down next to Damon's chair as I sit further back on a towel. It's his second Gathering.

> "How was Twiztid?" He asks.

> "They were good,' Damon says, 'but they only played for fifteen minutes."

> "Yeah, that's what I heard," Richie says, then asks how the new CD sounded.

> "We didn't listen to it." Damon replies.

Richie asks what we thought of the Psychopathic Rydas and other bands who played. Eventually, the conversation comes around to how everyone hocks something out here.

> "At concerts and festivals we've gone to, there's always a bunch of parasites that sit around and beg for change, booze, drugs or whatever. Here nobody's even asked me for a cigarette. It's really a shock," I say.

"Everybody here is a hustler,' Richie responds, 'everybody out here has some kind of caper going on."

We tell Richie that's one of the first things we noticed—how everything constantly turns over here. Lightly-used ICP jerseys sell for drugs, which sell for booze, which sell for glow-in-the-dark hatchets, which sell for titty flashes. The ingenuity of the Juggalos resourcefulness amazes us. While most of the cash floats up to the top—obvious from the amount of HatchetGear we see at the Gathering—quite a bit still floats around from Juggalo to Juggalo on a lower ring of commerce. The program we received about the Gathering listed a lot of restricted items, glass bottles and the like. Since it's our first Gathering, we did our best to not bring anything on the restricted list, for fear we wouldn't get in. Most concerts or festivals of this size overflow with rules and regulations and organizers stringently adhere to them order to avoid lawsuits, but upon arrival to the Gathering it's clear nobody actually gives a damn. Everybody returning knows they can do whatever the hell they want, so the Juggalos save and scam up enough money to get down here and then ball whatever they can to cover their costs once they arrive.

It's as much a part of the culture as ignoring everything else in the program—from no throwing things, to no fireworks, to no glass bottles. Just about every "rule" proves irrelevant. People set up booths hustling everything one might forget, from sunscreen, to ice cold beer, to blunt wraps. This part of Juggalo culture may trickle down from it's hip-hop roots, but maybe it stems more from the fact Juggalos are usually underclass. It's not something I'm used to; I'm used to the parasitic element of counterculture–crusty punks and hippies who come out to leech everything they can, from beer, to cigarettes, drugs, and change. They travel from festival to festival all year round to sit in one spot with busy foot traffic and beg for other people's stuff, and I have come to expect it. Too lazy to join society, they come up with some kind of wishy-washy, pseudo-political justification to plague the fringes. Out at the Gathering, however, nobody so much as asks me for a cigarette. Everybody here is indeed, as Richie stated, a hustler.

"I couldn't buy a ticket, so me and my ninjas snuck in here. A lot of ninjas do,' a Juggalette joins in the conversation, 'since I've been out here ninjas have been taking care of me with food 'n' shit."

Hearing her story shows there's definitely something to be said for the Juggalo Family. Since everyone considers themselves Family and there are few leaches out here, the 'los who ask for a bit of help get what they need, from each according to their abilities, to each according to their needs. There's a dignity the Juggalos have in this sense I have yet to see anywhere else.

However, there is a limit to the hustling, and that's when it cuts into the profits of ICP. As Damon and I walk back to the van from Lake Hepatitis, we see some Juggalos call out a dumpy, creep-mustached, middle-aged man about twenty years older than them.

"You guys want to buy some stickers?" the older man asks, displaying bootleg Hatchetman stickers in his hand.

"Fuck you, get the hell out of our Gathering," one of the Juggalos shouts at him.

"I'll go where ever I want," he responds.

"Nobody wants your shit, fuck off!" yells the other 'lo.

I like plenty of bands, really like them, but I give a damn whether or not they lose money on some stickers. But Juggalos learn to care about the profits that go back to ICP, even if it's a fraction of a cent from some lousy stickers.

The Insane Clown Posse Seminar

Seminar, noun. A small group, or course, for advanced study.
- The New American Webster Handy College Dictionary

A crowd of thousands stand under the blazing sun, amassed around the Seminar Tent. The Juggalos wrap so thickly around the outside of the tent I can't see those inside taking up the hay bale seating, let alone the stage. Inside, Violent J and Shaggy 2 Dope hold their seminar.

I listen for a while as they talk about their upcoming tour and CD's coming out on Psychopathic Records. They talk about the wrestling auditorium they are building in Detroit. They just promote and promote for most of an hour. Then Violent J gives away fly shoes to 'los who correctly answer trivia questions about ICP. According to him, the shoes are worth $800 and he's worn the pair only a hand full.

"If you wash them up they'll be fresh," he says.

I think about how much an $800 pair of shoes might fetch me on Ebay. Could I get more if Violent J once wore them?

The next thing they talk about is throwing shit.

"Who thinks this year's no throwing shit policy is lame? Who thinks that?" Violent J asks.

A big cheer comes up from the crowd, mixed with some booing.

"Who's for this year's no throwing shit rule?"

Another bigger cheer goes up.

"I know everybody's talking about throwing shit at Tila Tequila..." Violent J goes on.

Some "WHOOP! WHOOPS!" come up from a good portion of the crowd.

"I want y'all to think about this," Violent J continues.

"Hey, I'm trying to fuck that bitch. She's lame, but she's hot." Shaggy butts in, his clown grin taking on a weird predatory context.

"We brought her here with the intentions of seeing something you don't see everyday,' Violent J explains, 'and that's Tila Tequila up there rapping. You're gonna do what you want to do and we're gonna love you regardless, but we just want you to know..."

"And I'm trying to fuck that bitch!" Shaggy repeats.

"And if you throw shit at her, there's no chance Shaggy's gonna fuck her. You can guarantee that," says Violent J

"You get the logic,' Shaggy says, pantomiming with a swing of his arm, 'I'll throw my dick at her."

"And we want Shaggy to be able to fuck that bitch," Violent J says, reiterating their instructions.

The Juggalos agree with some "WHOOP! WHOOPS!"

"And if you throw shit at the wrestling,' Violent J continues, 'you're going to make the matches shitty, man."

Shaggy and Violent J explain why it's not cool to throw stuff at the wrestler's, that it makes the ring wet and makes wrestler's screw up their moves.

With that final point the seminar ends and a huge "WHOOP! WHOOP!" rises from the Juggalos.

'That's it?" I wonder to myself.

With the seminar over, I move on to watch Juggalo Class Wrestling, ICP's wrestling league. ICP spares no skrilla on the Hard Knox Wresting stage. It's elevated and surrounded by bleachers and even boasts a long red runway for wrestler's to strut down as they make their entrance. I sweat in the heat and swig on a jug of water as I watch the match. A bad guy wrestler in a police uniform who calls himself Officer Colt Cabana taunts the crowd,

> "I pulled a bunch of you faggots over on the way in and I made my quota and then some."

The crowd boos him in mock distaste. He goes on pointing the butt of a Mag Light into the crowd,

> "I will now start the first annual Gathering of the Juggalos D.A.R.E concept. Keep children and Juggalos off of drugs. I dare you to get a job. I dare you to get out of your mother's basements. I dare you to go to a dentist, young kid. I dare you to stop sucking everyone's dick young lady. I dare you to get a haircut..."

The crowd screams epithets back at the wrestler.

> "And I dare you to stop being a Mexican!" Colt shouts and points.

> "OOOOHHHH!" The Juggalos retort in unison.

Racism gets 'em. Colt turns it onto the referee,

> "And you call yourself an official. This is a Black man in charge. I can only assume you are the sole reason for the drugs spread all around this campground."

Now the Juggalos just go crazy booing and ranting, shouting back at Officer Colt. Bottles fly at the stage, but other 'los regulate these shit-throwing ninjas quickly. They're singled out with a quick chant of "DON'T THROW SHIT!" barely interrupting the wrestler's script.

> "I believe each and every one of you Juggalos are human pieces of shit and when I'm done with arresting you I will arrest Violent J and Shaggy 2 Dope. I will put them in jail and I will fuck them in their ass, because that's what a good cop does."

He presses a thick, pink, rubber dildo to the crotch of his khakis, walks to the turnbuckle, stands on the ropes, thrusts his hips and gets some laughs from the crowd. Am I the only one here wondering where the hell the dildo came from? Because I didn't notice it before. Did a Juggalo throw it on the stage? Or did he have it stashed somewhere? Not that it matters, but even with all of the rule-breaking Juggalos throwing things and ranting, the whole thing is an act and an exchange between the audience and the wrestler. It's not odd that a "bad guy" wrestler at the Gathering of the Juggalos portrays a cop and a racist, but it does take on a surrealistic quality. It makes a point of the freedom the Juggalos feel at the Gathering by setting up of a parody of authority besides ICP, and the fact the Juggalos get really worked up when the wrestlers character revealed his racism says something about the Family. The Family doesn't truck with racists. ICP won't have it. The Juggalos take their songs about fucking up racists and "bigots" (I put bigot in quotes, because it only seems to only apply to those who discriminate against class or People of Color) seriously.

The term "post-racial" comes to mind. It's one which always offended me because it's used to get away with putting disguised racism right out there in the open, and a cheap way to deny the fact People of Color still face oppression. I'm hesitant to use the term "hipster" because the term means something different to everyone, but I can't help but think of the track-bike riding, PBR swilling faction of wealthy hipsters who recently discovered the Juggalos as something else to make fun of. Hipsters famously make ironic racist jokes to come off as edgy, and then call anyone who disagrees a "pussy" because they "can't take it." Meanwhile, they live on trust funds, gentrify neighborhoods, and basically live a life of wealth while everybody else struggles to put food on the table. It would take an idiot not to notice racism and to say it's over, just like it would take an idiot not to notice poverty; but wealth hinders empathy.

If I've ever seen anything post-racial, it's this Dark Carnival. Everyone here is considered Family. Everybody here is a "floob" and equal. Everyone has similar ethics as dictated by ICP. Colt Cabana isn't being ironic, he's playing a role, being the bad guy wrestler. We're supposed to hate him and when the good guy comes out we root for him. Of course, Colt knows what gets the Juggalos riled up and he works it. Outside of Gathering, a cop throwing down race bombs offend the Juggalos, but there are no cops here. He's just a bad guy wrestler and all the 'los and 'lettes mock him in racial harmony. Nothing is misunderstood. No sensitivities or sensibilities are fucked with. WHOOP! WHOOP!

This exemplifies one of the more positive ways Insane Clown Posse use their influence. Since they reach so many dispossessed white folks, they've likely swayed a lot of uneducated people to overcome their prejudiced backgrounds. Everything ICP says stands as the indisputable truth, from soda pop to politics. Violent J has done well by this; ICP claims they open a lot minds through their strong anti-racist stance and some Juggalos agree; their minds opened up just because they respect Violent J and Shaggy.

Insane Clown Posse reaches people where they are. Since most of their followers are disenfranchised, they feel it when ICP raps about killing child molesters and wife beaters and rich people. Hearing ICP rap about these issues may be the first time they've heard such familiar issues addressed in a way that allows them to release their rage.

For a moment, I slip back into the past. I think about driving my best friend Tammy around when we were teenagers. I think about pulling my shitty Chevy LeBaron over on the side of a dusty rural route and holding her after we pulled away from her uncle's trailer.

"The guy who raped me was in there," she ran out bawling.

I knew the story already. She had already told me about how her older uncle, whom she looked up to, had given his twenty-something drunk friend permission to rape her.

"Go do it," he said, too drunk to move from the couch. It was something I was reminded of every time she hit seek on the radio when that mic-stand humping, jerk-off, Stephen Tyler of Aerosmith came on caterwauling about Janie having a gun and needing to "run, run away from the pai-ai-ain."

Plenty of heroes for the people exist in the history of popular music and plenty of rock stars speak for the poor and the wretched of the earth, but none of them hit them quite like Violent J and Shaggy. It all adds up to one thing–ICP never quit speaking to the poor in their language. They gave them pride in themselves, in being "scrubs" and "floobs." Then they gave them a Family and a Wicked Clown mask to shield them. Almost everything the Juggalos deal with ICP has lived through. Violent J and Shaggy have that authenticity, the same authenticity which kept me from ever-asking Tammy why she loved her uncle so much. Or why she would ever want to go back into that awful trailer again. Then I realize how easily I'm thinking about all this shit while I'm watching a guy in a cop uniform wrestle a guy in a green and yellow jumpsuit after tossing a dildo into the crowd. And I realize why I'm here. Not the reasons I told you I came out here for, but why I'm here. And I realize I just broke the code.

Though amused by the vulgar pre-match blustering, I quickly bore of the match once it starts. I watched wrestling as a kid and I looked forward to checking it out here. What other event would I end up at that includes professional wrestling in the ticket price? But without all of the different camera angles of television it just seems slow and tedious. The wrestlers take forever to set up their moves, and the execution of them hardly impresses. Don't get me wrong, it's well done, top-of-the-line pro wrestling, but I've outgrown the whole shtick and the weather makes it just too damn hot for entertainment. No matter how much water I drink I feel miserable and nauseous. Finally, it all gets to me and I run around to the back of the bleachers and puke my guts out, distracting a few Juggalos from the match and they shout, "WHOOP! WHOOP!"

Still dizzy from the heat, I head back to the van. I notice the Juggalos packing into the merch booth. A line of them snake out into the hot sun outside the autograph tent. Early this morning they started lining-up around it, clutching posters, CDs, T-shirts, and whatever else, to get signed by Psychopathic Records artists and other guests of the Gathering. But now trash has taken over. The brown straw grass of the grounds, ugly before, is now completely obscured by garbage. Faygo bottles, empty nitrous balloons, discarded glowsticks, half-eaten elephant ears, greasy, marrowy bones of Bitch Beaters, paper plates, tons of swag from Wicked Shit rappers, broken things and glow-in-the-dark novelties that no longer glow in the dark litter the ground. The Juggalos seem oblivious to this eyesore of trash, but I can't help noticing it's everywhere. Sure we're out on some crappy biker land, brown and brittle and dried out and no one's really here for camping, but still, the amount of litter grosses me the fuck out.

I find Damon sitting in his collapsible lawn chair in the shade with his bad foot propped up inside the open van door, drinking beer and drawing Juggalos.

"Hey, one of you ninjas got a lighter," a Juggalette says, coming up to our van. "Hey, that's cool,' she says looking over Damon's shoulder at his drawing, 'you're awesome."

I dig a lighter out of the van, hand it to her and she sparks up a bowl. She holds out to me, so I decline, telling her I have a piss test coming up.

"Aw, that sucks, ninja," she says and passes it to Damon who hits it and hands it back.

She's from Wisconsin, a town I've never heard of, and it quickly slips my mind.

"I'll talk to you 'los" she says and walks off to her nearby camp with a "WHOOP! WHOOP!"

"WHOOP! WHOOP!" we shout back.

We crack open a couple of beers, wash down the Percocet Damon scored earlier from a teenager, and chill out by the van until the drugs kick in and the heat gets more tolerable. Juggalos come by–most just shouting "WHOOP! WHOOP!" but a few stop by to say hello. Nathan and Samantha stop by and tell us about the Miss Juggalette contest.

"There was a Juggalette who was having dudes wrap dollar bills around their dicks and then she came around and took the dollars off with her mouth,' Samantha says, 'but then, she got beat out by a squirter who was squirting in guys' faces."

Jared and Mark drop in and out, as their camp butts up against ours. Jared tells us of the time he rapped with Shock G from Digital Underground a long time ago.

"They asked the crowd if anybody could rap. Well, I used to at the time, so my buddy pointed me out and I got pulled up on the stage by Shock G. I just picked out two girls at the front of the stage that seemed to be digging it and starting rapping to them, pretending they were the whole audience. I was pretty nervous." He smiles, taking another pull of his blunt and blowing the sweet fruity scent through the air.

As he talks, we try to figure out how to get Mark back into the Gathering. Last night he ripped his wristband off while he tripped on acid. Crystal, a frail blonde with a nasty scar that curves up from her mouth for nearly three inches, is trying to help find a solution. She bribed gate security to let her in without a wristband by offering him several cans of beer. Then she cut off her own wristband and gave it to Mark so he could get in. Now we're trying to find a way to attach her wristband to Mark's wrist. We use my pocketknife to cut up a promo sticker of some clown rapper and tape the wristband together. Crystal doesn't really seem motivated for any reason other than to help Mark out. They don't even appear to know each other, she's just camped nearby. They go to the gate to try it out and it works, then come back and we all hang out. We talk. We laugh and tell stories. The sun will soon set and I'm feeling pretty drunk.

Overall, I like the Juggalos. Most of them are nice folks. A lot of them I would even call gentle, as people who've been kicked around a lot and don't fit in with the world often are. Take Jared, he's not much different from the guy who might live in your apartment building or down the block, the guy who occasionally swings by with a six-pack. He talks about a lot more than Wicked Shit, making him easy to find common ground with. I could easily see Damon and me befriending someone like Jared outside of the Gathering. But Juggalos like Jared are the minority. The difference is the level of dedication and this where it gets tricky. Most Juggalos entrench themselves in the lifestyle, so for every Juggalo like Jared who I talk to, I talk to many more who are just as friendly, but much harder to relate to. The disconnect that draws them apart so much from the rest of society is just about all of them are true believers. They live, eat and breathe the Dark Carnival. They alienate themselves from the rest of society, and the unaffiliated, such as myself, because Violent J, Shaggy and Psychopathic Records filter everything in their world. When a Juggalo meets an open-minded outsider, they believe it crucial for them to explain the Family's importance. Juggalos aren't proselytizers though, they just want respect from where they're coming from and are usually stoked just to talk to a listening ear. I can say I've been treated with far more respect here than the world ever granted them. I'm not saying I haven't been met with some antagonism and distrust when a Juggalo learns I'm not a part of the Dark Carnival, but for the most part, when I tell them I'm a "punk," they think I came into that culture for the very same reason they became Juggalos and there lies a common understanding. We may differ in every other way, but the fact we're misfits and outcasts holds weight. Or maybe I just haven't told them enough about myself.

> "You're the only one who's given us a chance,' a Juggalo named Brian tells me, 'most just want to take us at a surface level."

This may hold true, but unlike a lot of people with counter-culture roots me and Damon willingly admit no matter how goofy the Juggalo aesthetic may seem to us, we come from a similar place, and maybe that makes it easier for us to understand the Juggalos. We too are familiar with shocking imagery, as well as take pride in being marginalized from our time spent in punk rock. We didn't listen to Psychopathic Records, but we did listen to psychopaths like G.G. Allin, who stabbed himself with broken glass and threw shit on the audience. And Richard Hell went on stage wearing a collared shirt with "please kill me" painted on it, wearing his inner turmoil on his sleeve. Of course, plenty of punks distinctly hate the Juggalos, placing themselves on a pedestal because their culture has the propensity to be more intellectual and more culturally relevant. But it's hard to deny the similarities between the wickedness of the Dark Carnival and the filth of punk. Maybe the smugness relates to punk's ties to the larger counter-culture, from anarchism to zines/small press to simply dropping out and living off the grid. Maybe it's just because punk carries more meaning and depth as a springboard to larger things. Maybe it's just because it's better art.

I'm reminded of my train ride to Louisville to meet up with Damon. I shared a seat with young Korean guy whom I befriended. He just spent a semester in Vancouver, Canada learning English and spoke it pretty well for only knowing it for such a short amount of time. The two of us hung out in the lounge car with some other travelers, and I talked about the Juggalos and my intentions behind attending their Gathering. I'm not sure how much he followed, as I tend to talk fast, but he understood enough to ask how someone like him, foreign with limited knowledge of American Culture, would be accepted out there. At the time, I couldn't answer that question, but now I think he would be welcome at the Gathering. The Juggalos are always on the defense because everything they care about is so reviled, but someone from a foreign culture who knows absolutely nothing about them would be just the kind of person to bring their guard down, and they'd probably feel compelled to show him a really good time.

Following the "most hated band in the world," though is a big responsibility. A couple of Juggalos threatened to kick my ass out here after finding out I'm not a Juggalo. It was always when they were in a group and more clannish. Mostly, though, the Juggalos are cool. It's the Juggalos who have a lot more going on in their lives like Jared that we relate to, but we've found they aren't very common.

As I've mentioned before, Insane Clown Posse lucked out and built an entire career around stuff they were into as kids, but the weird part is how the Juggalos just eat it up. Everything the ICP is down with, Juggalos obsess over. The Juggalos lack complexity and individuality, buying the whole wicked dream. I'm hard-pressed to find a Juggalo who will say, "I love ICP, but I think Faygo is too sweet and besides pop is an unhealthy beverage," or "I love my Fam but honestly, I'm more of a fan of Russian literature than wrestling," or "I'm a Juggalette, but I find Faygo wet T-shirt contests to be degrading to women." No, everything trickles top down from couple of charismatic clown leaders and the Juggalos follow. This level of unquestioning adherence to ICP only builds upon itself, because the more the Juggalos get behind it, the more they alienate themselves from the rest of the world and seek respite in the Family.

Last year I read *The Game*, a book about pick-up artists, an underground group of nerdy dudes who shell out thousands of dollars to gurus who teach them how to use neuro-linguistic programming and pop-psychology to score with lots of chicks. The author, Neil Strauss, was a successful rock journalist who had trouble meeting women, so he became involved and eventually became one of the top pick-up gurus in the country. When he began holding seminars and workshops to teach other repressed bro-hams and spurned yuppies to be "respected social artists" he became a millionaire almost overnight.

The leaders of this subculture, not unlike Violent J, had a whole lot to give. For them, they offered the promise of self-esteem, poise and grace in social settings and, finally, lots of babes. These gurus are worshiped by their followers, and as gurus are rarely criticized, the pick-up artists get completely behind anything they say. The pick-up artists are marketed to constantly through e-books and training courses and web conferences. Some of these things cost up to a few grand, but it seems a small price to pay to date models and strippers and to be the envy of ones peers. Also, at the bottom, a supportive community sprang up where they may get together in person and online to discuss strategy and routines to pull in women. As one progresses in their "game" they start to make a name for themselves.

I'm reminded of this book when I witness the Juggalos and their anti-critical belief in the Psychopathic Records Family and ICP. Anything ICP says is taken as gospel. I run into little trouble with the Juggalos out here when they discover I'm not a Juggalo, but I hear rumors of forty of fifty Juggalos almost mobbing someone who said something bad about ICP and the offender only got out of it when his buddy ran to the car threatening to pull out his gun. I feel things could just as easily go south for Damon and me if we say the wrong things to the wrong Juggalos about their leaders. Both Violent J and pick-up gurus like Strauss posses a similar charisma that makes people listen to and follow them. They both offer community, something bigger than themselves to belong to, as well as spirituality and ethics. And let's not forget fun. But ICP stops there. With pick-up gurus, they give back feelings of self-betterment, ascension and "empowerment." They basically take the tenets of self-help psychology and apply it to areas of life where it's lacking in their students and providing them with a supportive community of peers. ICP doesn't have a problem marketing this million-dollar underground industry to their followers, and instead, with so much to offer, they feel the ends justify the means. The psychology empowers these dorks to make more of their lives and to live lives to impress the women they want to lay.

Both ICP and the pick-up gurus also share a huge understanding of marketing and promotion. They found something that works and they know how to milk it for all it's worth. The common ground stops here though–pick-up artist subculture encourages the very best (on the level of success, if not ethics) out of their followers. The other camp encourages their followers to watch wrestling, drink generic pop and listen to Vanilla Ice. Both encourage an enormous amount of materialism, but at least the pick-up artists sell a dream that's possible to attain by following their pop-psychology media. ICP only encourages Juggalos to buy another T-shirt, another CD, and another Hatchetman necklace. Wicked Shit.

"The Juggalos make me think of this book I read called *The Starfish and the Spider.*" My friend Carlos tells me when I return to my home in Seattle.

"It describes two kinds of leadership. One is top-down, which is the spider, and the other is the starfish which is decentralized leadership. If we break off the leg of a starfish, another grows in its place, and with top down leadership, if we take off the head the body dies. The starfish relies on no central leadership so it's hard to stop or to contain. It's something like Burning Man, which goes on to empower people to make their own festivals like Mutant Fest or exposes them to art or maybe autonomy."

Carlos thought of this theory because he felt like Insane Clown Posse operates on the spider top-down model of leadership. They may use an out-dated model, but nobody could argue that it doesn't work. It's actually baffling how well it works.

Juggalo Island

On Juggalo island/We can be one./ Let our nuts hang by the water./
On Juggalo island, we can have fun. We can let go, by the water.
-Insane Clown Posse

ICP recently finished shooting a video for their song "Juggalo Island" at the Gathering. Like "Miracles," ICP released "Juggalo Island" for the Juggalos, but also as an insular reply to the accidental notoriety they received for "Miracles." It's a sappy number about how great it would be if all the Juggalos inhabited their own island where they could "all be one" and just "let their nuts hang by the water," leaving the world–the rest of the world who hate them–behind. The video features footage of Juggalos making homemade water slides, swinging off ropes into Hepatitis Lake, grilling hot dogs and dancing. Just the Family with some Psychopathic Records rappers mixed in–no models, no celebrities, just Juggalos. Fucking unity, how does that work?

> "It's every motherfucker here that makes the Gathering worth it, man. I remember the first time with, like, Juggalos, whether they're, I dunno, fucking mushroom-heads, whatever, dude. It just makes it all worth it. First time, the greatest day in the world. Alright?" says a Juggalo known as Jaymo.

A lot of the Juggalos talk about the Gathering being their conversion, but for many, it happened while being hosed down with Faygo at an ICP concert. The Family is very real and valid, it's something so strong that they commit their entire lives to it.

Just like the lower ring of commerce, there seems to be a lower ring of Clown Love, one that hits on a deeper and more real level than the adoration Juggalos have for ICP and Psychopathic Records, and I really feel it in the air here.

> "If I see someone wearing an ICP shirt that isn't a Juggalo, I'll tell them to take that shit off, dog, that's my Family, man. They'll be all, 'oh OK, my bad' and it's cool, but that's how I feel about it," another Juggalo tells me.

I'm starting to learn the Family strongly draws one to become a Juggalo and in the process one picks up the Dark Carnival, not the other way around. The Dark Carnival adapts and moves fluidly, akin to how the Family accepts other Juggalos. The camaraderie of the Family makes all of it appealing–ICP, the Dark Carnival, and Wicket Shit.

> "It reminds me of an old Gypsy folk saying,' I hear from a friend on my return, 'it goes something like this, 'In the enemy's language, the lie is the rule.'"

My friend is reminded of the saying in context to Juggalos and how their culture and customs confuse outsiders and the way their imagery and aesthetics don't reflect their mainstream counterparts or have roots to the larger counter-cultural alchemy. It seems once a Juggalo becomes involved with the Dark Carnival they enmesh themselves further and further into it and withdrawn from the outside world. The Family replaces everything and they listen to every word ICP tells them, making information from anywhere else less and less relevant. I've heard people say the Dark Carnival sounds like a cult. I disagree. After all, no one's forcing anyone to stay, telling them to reject their other family and friends, nor, to my knowledge, shunning them if they leave. I prefer to call them cultish, because they certainly perpetuate cultish elements, for instance, the way they speak their own language and the way Family permeates their entire existence. Learning this about the Family clears up a lot of what I fail to understand in the lyrics, as Juggalos apply meaning after they feel Clown Love. I fail to get it, because I haven't opened my mind to get it.

> "It's bliss, it's like nirvana and pretty much like a version of Heaven, I guess. It can be Heaven depending on who you are. If you're into religion it is Heaven. It's whatever makes you happy," Fuckstick offers his opinion about Clown Love.

> "Everybody has their own outlook on Clown Love,' Bubbles tells me, 'you can't just take it from two random Juggalos."

> "Honestly, you're gonna have to interview every Juggalo,' Kentucky tells me, 'because it's different for everyone."

A series of vague, violent quasi-religious lyrics compromise the Dark Carnival until one feels the Clown Love. That's why one doesn't meet many Insane Clown Posse fans, only Juggalos, because to even put a toe into it, they've got to get it. One has to open their mind to get it. The Wicked Clown must appeal to one enough for them to look into it in the first place, but then when one becomes involved, when they drop their first hit of acid at an Insane Clown Posse show or get sprayed down with Faygo, the moment is imprinted. Their body remembers it. WHOOP! WHOOP!

The sun starts to go down, Damon and I are lit up on Percocet and whiskey and heading to the Main Stage to check out 90's G-funk rapper Warren G. The crowd tallied around 15,000 last night, but right now the crowd looks pretty sparse and the Juggalos keep themselves busy by throwing trash all over the place. Damon and me laugh as the trash flies all around, pelting us. Ahead of us a backyard-style wrestling *Battle Royale* breaks out—ninjas just start beating each other with folding chairs and whatever else they find. I pull a Juggalo aside for a photo. He wears a HatchetGear hockey jersey embroidered with a dark, faceless hooded figure with the words 'The Wraith' emblazoned across the back. An open gash drips blood on his forehead, and he flashes the devil sign and sticks his tongue out for the picture. We giddily take pictures of the Juggalos acting the most outrageous in their clown make up, and they gladly ham it up for the camera. We put ourselves in the pictures with them and they throw up Wicked Clown hand signs. Juggalos love having their pictures taken. It's funny, though, because these photos won't be used for my book—no, the pictures document our trip for ourselves. And right now we are having one hell of a time.

'How long has it been since Warren G actually did a show?' crosses my mind as I dodge Faygo bottles and punch giant beach balls flying toward me, and I realize I'm actually enjoying the worst mainstream rapper of the nineties…I mean, I fucking hate Warren G.

"Hey Ninja, I like that Crass tattoo,' A tall, muscular, Latino Juggalo says, pointing to Damon's shoulder, 'I love that band."

It's the first time we cross an actual cultural divide between us and the Juggalos. Crass was a radical Anarchist band from the seventies in England, revolutionary and completely anti-state to the point of irritating arrogance, most famous for radicalizing and politicizing several generations of young people and promoting communalism and revolution.

The crossover into familiar territory shocks me and I wish I could take the ninja aside and ask him why he likes the band, how he discovered them and how it pertains to being a Juggalo. But instead, I say nothing. Damon makes small talk with him, asking him where he's from. He's from L.A., but I forget the importance of this when I'm struck on the shoulder with a near full can of beer.

"That was a full can of beer!" I shout to Damon, offended at the waste of alcohol. The punks would never waste a perfectly good beer.

"Get over it," Damon says. And I stop thinking of such things.

The Carnival

Carnival don't fuck around/Fire up the tilt-a-whirl And we'll see you all in hell/They all die/They All Die/Round and round and round you go/Yo, the dark carnival will never die.
-Insane Clown Posse

Darkness sets in and we decide to ride the Tilt-A-Whirl. We stand in line behind a chubby girl with a tattoo in the middle of her back; the inscription "Skrilla" sits in the middle of banner sandwiched between two Hatchetmen. I ask to take a picture of it and she lets me, the flash bringing out the sunburn on her back. I have a moment of clarity as I look at the picture on my camera screen, the disembodied skin of a person whose clown name may or may not be Skrilla. I'm uncomfortable with taking it and put the camera away for awhile.. We get on the ride and a Juggalette turns from her seat in front of me and says,

"What's up, 'lo?"

She's pretty, with long blonde hair. On her forearm is a stylish tattoo of an old style compass one might see on a treasure map, and around her neck she wears a leather bondage choker with long loops hanging from it.

"Are you enjoying the Gathering?" She asks.

"Yeah, I'm having a really good time," I say as things start spinning.

She tells me her name and the location of a party her camp is throwing tonight, but both slip my mind. The ride stops and Damon and I stumble dizzily off it towards each other, the drugs and booze all twisted up in our stomachs. Damon tells me he'll meet me back at the van and wanders off to puke his guts out for the next hour. Determined to press on, I head to the Midway and buy a corn dog to settle my own queasiness. It does the job, and, fully recovered, I head to the Drug Bridge to mingle.

I dodge golf carts and golf carts narrowly dodge me. "WHOOP! WHOOP!" Juggalos from the carts shout and I laugh and yell it back to them. Now that the sun is down and Psychopathic bands are about to go on, more and more 'lo's and 'lettes paint themselves up. The evil grins fit the party atmosphere.

I pass one of the carnival games. A Juggalo and a carny stand in front of a dunking tank. On the dunking tank sits a topless woman and the two men haggle over the price of the balls the Juggalo needs to throw to dunk the girl.

"Came I take her out to Hepatitis Lake with me if I win?" The Juggalo asks.

"Yeah, sure, sure, you can take her."

"Uh-uh! No!" The girl shouts from her place on the tank.

Life fills the Drug Bridge. Dealers holler out what they're peddlin'. Buyers barter. A pear-shaped Juggalette offers titty-flashes to sweeten the deal on a dub sack. Deals are made everywhere so everyone can roll, trip or get high for the show. Juggalos pass by holding handmade signs of the drugs they're selling. I'm sitting with Kentucky just shooting the shit. I genuinely like Kentucky, his energy and enthusiasm, and since this is his house, I let him do most of the talking. He's a lot younger than me and I wonder how his life's going to unfold, and I hope the best for him and every Juggalo out here. Directly across from us, leaning on the opposite rail, a short guy holds his own large sign that proclaims, "I just wanted to waste your time."

"What do you think of WHOOP! WHOOP!?" Kentucky asks me.

"Well, I think it's kind of goofy but it's seems to have it's purpose. Ya know? For instance, those times when everybody's partying and some dude comes up to you all fucked up and babbling and shouting, or whatever. He's just having a good time, but you don't know what to say? Well, you can just say WHOOP! WHOOP! You know? Times like that"

"Yeah, I know what you're saying," Kentucky laughs.

Connecting with Kentucky is easy, as I think humanizing someone throws a rope-a-dope to your ego. So often enough we avoid it like a disease, but if it happens it's really not so bad. It's calming even, to strip down your arrogance, leaving only the bare essence of what makes us human. It brings people around to the facts we all struggle and life is damned hard. I think about my own shortcomings. I'm fucked up, my mind awash in pills and booze to calm all my self-doubt about jumping into this project, about chucking all journalistic integrity out the window. As I chill with Kentucky, I think of others I've met out here. Not everybody, hell, I've found plenty of fucking dumbshits out here, but everybody who's cool, who respected me. And I wonder about the true nature of betrayal is. Is it intent or lack of honesty?

A guy in a tie-dye shirt with long, gray, balding hair wanders across the Drug Bridge. He's gazing wall-eyed at everything around him, tripping balls.

"Hey, what's up?" Kentucky asks him.

He gives a dazed smile and a slow languorous wave and Kentucky says,

"WHOOP! WHOOP!"

"That old dude's fucked up," I say.

"That's Gallagher," Kentucky tells me, the seventies comedian famous for taking sledgehammers to watermelons.

"Chase him down and I'll get a picture of you with him," I tell Kentucky.

He does and I snap the picture–Kentucky with a big grin and his arm around Gallagher frying on acid. Then I head back to camp to catch up to Damon and re-up on booze. He's chilling around the van shooting the shit with some Juggalos and drinking whiskey,

"Hey, I was hoping you'd make it back. That ride made me puke five times."

"This is Craven," he tells the 'los he's chilling with.

I flop down and smile to myself. I'm having a hell of a time, I'm with my best friend and 20,000 Juggalos in the middle of nowhere and I'm about to listen to clowns rap. I'm not sure any of this counts as journalism, but I'll be damned if I care right now.

A knife in my hand and I know what I expect of me/
The blood lust in the fear is what I'm lookin' for/Rush in my veins as I rush
and slowly bleed this whore /Its pure desire and it burns at me like fire/
Mercedes and a murder spree is what it takes to get me higher
-Boondox, Psychopathic Records Artist

The sun's gone down on all our drinking. Boondox, Psychopathic Records' backwoods, white boy rapper, plays on stage, his face clowned-up in black and white. The edges of his greasepaint jagged smile curve like a jack-o-lantern done in a tribal tattoo design. He rocks a cowboy hat and flannel and points his finger-gun into the crowd. The Juggalos throw theirs back up at him. "WHOOP! WHOOP!" They all yell. He kicks rhymes about moonshine and taking Ecstasy and stabbing, hacking up and asphyxiating anybody who fucks with him or Psychopathic. Or just anybody, period. "WHOOP! WHOOP!" Yells the crowd. And the booze, the pills and the Clown Love all kick in. I slide into the visceral night and start getting down. Damon and me shout along with the crowd. "WHOOP! WHOOP!" Painted-up clowns pass us joints. Faygo bottles, beer cans and all other projectiles fly about. Titties bounce this way and that. Just about everybody is rolling, tripping, or in some other way fucked the hell up! Total freedom! Nobody looks twice at Damon or me, and for all they know we're just down-ass 'los. And I don't know about you, but I don't want to be on my deathbed knowing I missed a chance to party with some folks just because they dressed like a bunch of clowns.

"FAM-UH-LEE! FAM-UH-LEE! FAM-UH-LEE!"

The crowd chants as Boondox, his hype man and the rest of the crowd leave the stage. My stomach flutters with pill buzz and humanity as I talk to Nick, a ninja with long unkempt brown hair from Boulder.

"I just think this is wonderful what you guys have. We just came out here to check it out but we're having a great time. I think it's incredible how you guys have this Family and stuff." I rave uncontrollably.

"We all take care of each other,' he says, 'it doesn't matter who you are or where you're from if you're down with the Hatchet then you're Family."

I may be leading the witnesses in my quest to figure out what the Juggalos are all about, but Juggalos I've talked with all say the same thing about the Family. None of them had anything before the Dark Carnival. They got down at ICP shows and felt the love, and then went to a Gathering. Nothing since matched this feeling of freedom, unity and love. They're down for life, hooked on the connection they feel. The Juggalo from Boulder gives me a hug. Now I get it. The Family doesn't question, or pull rank or cut itself into subgenres. It doesn't mire itself in politics or lack of politics. It's just freedom, man. For all of my participation in underground subcultures, I've never felt anything like this. It's more than a concert where you "feel the love in the room" and afterwards everyone goes on with their lives. For the Juggalos, the Family realness lasts.

As the night progresses, I slip even more into the Clown Love. Titties flash everywhere throughout the night. The "FAM-UH-LEE" chant never stops. Hands pass out drugs and booze everywhere. More backyard wrestling matches commence–flashlight wrestling matches and midget wrestling leagues. There are no narcs or security, and nothing to stop the non-stop hedonism except for other 'los and that only happens when someone really fucks up. FAM-UH-LEE!

"Ketamine," I yell at some point on the Drug Bridge, "does anybody have Ketamine?"

"Ketamine?" A thick Juggalette comes up to me. "You have Ketamine?"

"No, I was looking for it…"

"Aw, fuck," she says, visibly bummed.

"Me too," I say, "well, how about a hug?"

"Sure," she says and embraces me as Damon laughs over my shoulder.

I just hugged a Juggalette…I JUST HUGGED A JUGGALETTE!

As the hours of my conversion slide quickly by, I watch Kottonmouth Kings rap about weed and I see Violent J's cryptic spiritual band, The Dark Lotus, kick the knowledge. Damon and I catch a bit of the second stage and some of Vanilla Ice rapping, blessed with a new context for his Teenage Mutant Ninja Turtles II theme "Go, Ninja, Go." I vaguely recollect seeing some Juggalette rapping about weed and fucking people up, and I remember some fat guys making fun of me and moving on to another set of clown faces to bro-down with.

As the night goes on things fade in and out. I lose and find Damon as we wander drunkenly through the Dark Carnival. I miss L'il Kim, but see a very baked Tom Green get the crowd to repeatedly chant "chicken sandwich" before getting antsy and leaving. I see Gallagher several more times wandering around, frying on acid. I lose hours and hours I have no recollection of. I regret it later on as bad journalism, but I file it under the excuse that my intention was to get down like the 'los do. All I say to each Juggalo I meet is that I think they're great and the Family is one of the greatest things I've ever experienced.

In and out of rolling blackouts, gentle ninja hands and arms grab me out of the darkness.

"Hey ninja, are you OK? Do you need some water?" they ask.

Further down other 'los check up on me. Clown Love.

Near the van but not quite ready to fall out, I wander to other camps nearby and chat to a 'lo named Gore from Kansas. He sits around a gas camp stove, cooking a pan of Ramen. He's about eighteen and appears glad to talk to me.

"You want some?" he says leaning towards me with the pan.

"No, thanks," I say, and we continue to talk for a while.

"Yeah, most of us came from fucked up places, man. Never had families or had kind of fucked up families. The Dark Carnival, this is our Family. This is why we're here. "

"Before I got here...I'd read that Juggalos come from all sorts of...are widely...diverse. But so far it seems like you're all pretty poor folks, working class folks...you get what I'm...saying..."

"None of us have any money, ninja." Gore says seriously.

Around us the rest of his camp, a couple of Juggalos and a Juggalette, argue. Something about somebody throwing something at someone else. I'm not really paying attention, it's none of my business and sounds like some drunk bullshit to me.

"It's like to tonight, man, some shit went down,' he pauses, waving his fork at his arguing crew, 'it's not perfect, but this is where the love is, man."

Titties and Bricks:
Relation and Assimilation

Oooh (Areola!), Oooh (Areola!), Oooh (Areola!)/
That shirt came off and showed a...
Oooh (Areola!), Oooh (Areola!)
-Tech N9ne and 816 Boys

Smack that bitch right across the lips
cause she aint nothin but a filthy bitch
beat the freak in the head with a cinder block
blacken her eyes your lunatic tock
–Insane Clown Posse

How I managed to recover so well from last nights indulgent bacchanal I have no idea. It's almost noon and Damon and I have been camped out at Lake Hepatitis. Far too hot to sleep after the sun started to rise, we're been getting in and out of the grimy water all morning, the only escape from another sweltering day. The Juggalos strip the dock of the plastic barrels underneath, which keep it afloat. It's tethered to the bottom of Hepatitis Lake by a very long rope, and with fewer and fewer barrels holding it up, the dock is mostly submerged under water except for whichever corner is butting up, ballasted (or anti-ballasted) by whatever side the more obese Juggalos stand on.

Plastic bottles fly all about. When we get in the water we keep a constant eye out for bottles thrown by the beach 'los as the dock lurks around us under the water. If we're not looking a sunken corner of it will scoop us up.

> "Heads up, ninja!" We hear a Juggalo in the water near us say to his buddy.

Not paying attention, a really fat, shirtless, tattooed Juggalo gets nailed right in the head with a gallon-sized Faygo bottle. The bottle contains a mixture of lake water and the remains of the soda.

"Aw shit, I yelled 'heads up', man. You OK?" His friend says.

Without blinking an eye, he picks up the bottle and chugs from it.

"Man, I just don't give a fuck. I just want to fuck a bitch with AIDS so I can get skinny and die," he says after a swig.

Sitting on my towel, I jot the following quotations down in my journal:

"I'm going to waggle my dick in his eye."

Juggalette: "Have you ever had sex on videotape for money?"
Juggalo: "Well, not for money."

"I sprinkled some mushroom powder on my spaghetti when I was at my grandma's and almost lost my shit. It sucked, ninja."

"Blacky! Blacky! Black guy! Hey, Black!"

"I have Faygo titty and everybody want to see it."

"I'm keeping close track of all of the crazy shit I hear people say out here," I tell Damon.

Out in the water, a shirtless Juggalo in mirrored sunglasses rides a blue barrel floating in the water.

"Johnny Knoxville, I'm Johnny Knoxville," he shouts, arms and legs wrapped around the barrel as it bobs in the water.

"Did you write down, 'how about a hug?' " Damon says, mocking me for my Ketamine hug last night.

"Fuck you," I say back.

"Well, I paid five dollars to see a girl's titties last night,' he says, 'I guess that was my own version of the 'K hug'." he says.

He goes on to tell the story.

"So I was trying to chat this girl up. I was all 'hey, what's your name, I want to get to know you...or whatever and she says, 'you want to see my titties don't you' So I said, 'yeah, yeah, I do want to see your titties'. So she said, 'well I'll show you my titties if you buy my friends glowsticks. They're two for five bucks. So I did. That was my last five bucks."

Damon likes to consider himself "pro-sleaze." What he calls pro-sleaze I tend to call sexism, but of a disarming and perhaps childish nature. Then again, we all find ways to get around questioning our friends sometimes (and by proxy ourselves). Damon revels in all of the skin and flesh of the Gathering and I waver between ethical distance and journalistic immersion. I feel a bit of complicity, which I excuse in the name of new journalism, and we also take advantage of having no one here looking over our shoulders. Nevertheless, we could say we at least *know* how to act.

Titties are some of the most important attractions, commodities and subjects at the Gathering. The chant of "TIT-TIES! TIT-TIES!" constantly resounds the air. The 'los display signs at their camps saying "free shots for tits." Juggalos walk around with signs asking to see titties. Juggalettes carry around signs saying things like "See my tits $5.00, $4.00, $3.00." The lack of class and floobiness in these actions reveal much about the lack of empowerment not only with 'lettes, but within the subculture itself.

Another thing Damon and I notice is after 'los request, shout or barter for titty flashes, the lette's put them away and both parties move on. Very little flirtation or Juggalos kicking game occurs. The Juggalos act pretty awkward and shy around the 'lettes, and perhaps that's why they settle for just gawking at boobies for a few seconds and then moving on. Maybe the mating habits of Juggalos are more complex and I'm just not picking up on them, but from my distance the Juggalos present themselves as a bit shy and lacking social skills, even when completely surrounded by their own people. Although Psychopathic imagery appears hard and tough and violent, a lot of Juggalos just appear to be nerdy kids in evil paint.

Juggalos in relationships with 'lettes treat their partners noticeably well, often putting them on a pedestal. We've seen 'los actually carry their 'lettes into the green waters of Lake Hepatitis. They canoodle and sit apart from the rest of their group of 'los so their 'lettes get all of their attention. The Juggalos we see hooked up also tend to be in their late twenties and thirties and appear to have been together for a long time. So the Juggalettes are either disrespected as objects, murdered and sexually assaulted in songs, or treated with knightly chivalry when partnered up. The most revealing thing about a culture, a faith or a group of people of any sort is how they treat and respect women, and the way women demand respect within that milieu. It says something about the balance of power. When a culture itself empowers, the more marginalized involved will eventually demand a voice, some respect and the right to place within a group. A good example in my world are the Riot Grrrl and Queercore movements, where women and queer-identifying people stood up to the straight male dominance in punk, forcing their scenes to hear and recognize them.

Wicked Shit may be redheaded stepchild of rap, but it's no less guilty than larger hip-hop culture, with it's long-standing tradition of portraying women as bitches and hoes. But I'm here to talk about the Juggalo Family and, by proxy, Wicked Shit and both exhibit a garish and repulsive sexism. For the Juggalo Family a back door to body positivity and a resistance to the normal beauty standards opens. Most of this sentiment comes from the "if you're Fam, you're Fam" philosophy, so a Juggalette is attractive simply because they're a Juggalette. The idea of floob pride fits here, pride in being out cast and underdog. Fat girls jump at the chance to grind a pole and get positive reinforcement. Some ICP lyrics even show some love to the fat girls. Underneath it all lies an honest resistance to unnatural and unfair beauty standards.

"Hey, what's up?" Richie says, shirtless and dressed in swim trunks.

"Oh, hi, good morning,' Damon says, 'I was just busting Craven here's balls because he gave a girl a Ketamine hug last night," he says.

Richie looks puzzled. So he tells him the story and Richie chuckles.

"I heard Tila Tequila got a brick thrown at her last night," he says.

This is the first we hear of the attack. We ask him more questions and he tells us Tom Green jumped to her defense and got beat down, too. I immediately regret missing this juicy event as I wandered around fucked up and acting a fool the night before.

"Where in the hell is someone going to get a brick out here?" says Damon, gesturing to the lake, the field, the trees.

"I may be a jackass, but y'all busted my lip open," yells the Juggalo imitating Johnny Knoxville from the lake; someone just hit him with a rock during the bottle fight.

"Not cool," he mutters, climbing back onto his barrel as the trash continues flying and nobody really listens to him.

For all the talk about the Tila Tequila incident, we meet few Juggalos who actually saw anything. I realize that's what the big argument last night at Gore's camp was about, not inner-camp conflict. The upset 'lette chewed her 'lo out for being in on the Tila attack.

"This is where the story is," Damon says looking at the program.

Yeah, and I had every opportunity to watch it last night, but instead, I just ran around partying with Juggalos everywhere but the second stage. Floob.

"Hey, look," Damon says, holding the program out to me, and points to a picture of Tila's face.

"Brick!" He says and we laugh.

As the day progresses, we hear more and more rumors of the attack, each far more outrageous than the last. I'm still afraid to just come out and ask someone exactly who the hell Tila Tequila is! Since everybody here seems to know, I just assume I'm supposed to know, too. I don't want to out myself as a non-Juggalo by revealing my ignorance. I don't know that I should know Tila Tequila, but not because I hadn't done enough research on Wicked Shit, but, instead, because she's a D-list celebrity. And it turns out I do know Tila Tequila, I just haven't realized it yet. I caught clips of her show, *A Shot of Love with Tila Tequila*, in some bar or waiting room. Tequila, a media whore along the lines of Paris Hilton, is pretty much famous for being famous. A 4' 11" model with giant fake breasts, Tila appeared in Playboy at age eighteen and from there used sleaze to climb ladders until she landed a show on which a bunch of brain-dead douche bags competed to date her. It was enough to make her a minor celebrity, and with the help of some domestic disputes and controversy, she became a bit of a spectacle in the media. I thought it'd hurt my street cred to ask the Juggalos who she was, but, apparently, it's pretty hard not to know. And this highlights the Juggalos problem with her. They find her insulting to their Gathering, feel she is here to exploit them and she has no business at their underground, horrorcore rap festival. And they made sure she knew.

Me and Damon weren't the only ones naive to Tila. After the attack, ICP told the media they didn't even know her. They claimed the organizers only told them about a "hot bitch" who raps and they gave the go ahead. Tila Tequila and Insane Clown Posse both used negative attention to get where they are, as the more controversy they get the more people pay attention to them. It wouldn't surprise me if both sides went into this hoping for a spectacle, allowing Tila to stretch out her fifteen minutes. and Insane Clown Posse to throw another net of negative press out in to the world.

More information comes our way. We learn Tila wasn't pelted with a brick but with rocks–a whole lot of them. To make things worse, people also threw bottles of piss and feces at her. We even hear tell of a water-melon soaked in a port-a-potty all day being chucked at her. The crowd demanded she take her top off, shouting "show us your tits." She complied with this command while taunting the crowd, shouting, "I ain't going anywhere."

A few wrestlers guarded her from the onslaught, finally dragging her off the stage against her will. At that point things completely exploded and a mob of Juggalos chased her and her by-proxy bodyguards to her trailer and busted out the windows. The part about Tom Green, however, wasn't true; he just ran out onto the runway and did a stupid dance to de-escalate things. Nobody fucked with him. The Juggalos like Tom Green, but they see right through Tila and maybe even to some degree, unlike my initial assumption, Insane Clown Posse.

"It's more commercialized bullshit they're trying to bring in here, 'cause it seems like ICP is getting more and more commercialized," a Juggalo named Bill tells me.

"Man, it's part of a conspiracy to make Insane Clown Posse more mainstream,' his buddy says, backing him up, 'they've been doing this shit for a while. Like, they (Violent J and Shaggy) were on Aqua Teen Hunger Force and Squidbillies making fun of Juggalos."

He's referring to Cartoon Network's Adult Swim, a series of absurdist and ironic cartoons popular with college kids and stoners right now. My friends keep sending me the clips of the episodes with the Juggalo parodies and from what I've seen, they poke fun at the Family, not ICP.

"I've seen those,' I say, 'I didn't know that ICP was involved."

"You could tell it was their voices," he says with disappointed distaste.

A lot of Juggalos feel the Family has a bad enough reputation without adding in more bad press. It goes against the Family morality to attack a woman. They also worry about how it will play out in the press and affect their already bad reputation. They discuss the declining ethics of younger Family who don't understand the core meaning of the Family. Still, most of them feel little sympathy for the banal pop star who took shit and piss to the face.

"I would of left if I was there seeing it happen, but I was asleep. I wouldn't of participated 'cause that's just wrong in general," a Juggalo named Chris tells me

"It was funny. It was fucked up but it was funny. It shouldn't have happened. She just shouldn't be here, that's all," another says.

Damon and I take it with a bit of humor, too. A wealthy Hollywood dirtbag getting pelted with piss and shit somewhat amuses us too. Do we wish it hadn't of happened? Well, I guess nobody deserves to get rocks thrown at them, but like most of the Juggalos, we find it morbidly funny. I carry about as much sympathy for her as I would any other richie... Tom Cruise...Paris Hilton...Bret Michaels. Hell, I'd laugh if any of them got pelted with shit and rocks. I view them all as enemies of the people. Coming up in punk we also hold the mainstream in contempt–for wealth, power and the spectacle. We come at it from different angles, but the Juggalos and us both despise mainstream culture for similar reasons. The Juggalos want to stay raw and wicked and don't need mainstream attention. The mainstream Tila represents insults them, and they see her as another "richie," another one of the beautiful people, another insult to their lives of struggle. But this time she entered their house, their turf, and stomps arrogantly through the one place on earth they hold sacred. They rose to protect their community, and I respect this. It may be a wild and rash grab at empowerment, at taking control of their lives, to protect what they hold dear, misguided an attack as it was, it was an act of resistance to assimilation and co-optation.

Last night, the Juggalos proved themselves a force to be reckoned with. They may not all agree it was the right thing to do, but at least a thousand or so formed an unorganized attack on a moronic, falling reality-TV star. I once heard Ice-T say of the Gathering, "if this shit were political they'd shut it down." But what if Juggalos struck out against their own leaders, their own prophets, their own idols? The heroes who sell them overpriced trinkets and sate them with autographs? What if they took control? What if they turned on the "richies" in their own community rather than a four foot bimbo with breast implants?

I came out here to try and understand this essence of the Family, and last night I understood, at the same time the Juggalos attached Tila Tequila, I got down with the Clown. I felt the solidarity, the gory pastoral nature of the Gathering...Clown Love. This is the Kingdom of Heaven. Step correct.

Juggalos, Insane Clown Posse and Violence

*My ax is my buddy, we right planet's wrongs/Me and my ax leave bigots
dead on richie's lawns/My ax is my buddy, he never make me cry/
Me and my ax will leave a divot for your eye
-Insane Clown Posse.*

The Bomb Tent stands almost completely empty for Juggalo MC Kara-
oke. An event where 'los give CD's of their recordings to a stage hand
who plays them. Then they rap over their own voices and beats. The few
Juggalos in the tent pay little attention to the 'lo on stage, waiting their
own turn to rap. Each Juggalo who gets up raps breathlessly, falling behind their own recorded voices. Most of the rappers lyrics seem to add
up to "don't fuck with me," as one skinny 'lo after another replaces the
next on the stage.

"You fucking suck," says a voice amplified with a bullhorn from a golf
cart packed with ninjas.

They heckle each rapper who comes on the stage. A painted-up Juggalo
takes a plastic bottle to the face when he raps. He gets really pissed off
and starts ranting to his friends about how fucked up it is and how they
are bunch of Juffalos for throwing shit.

"Yeah, you were OK...not really," the heckler with the bullhorn mocks.

The rapper storms off and at that, the stage-hand mumbles something
like "All right, I'll see all of you clowns, later," and just takes off.

"Do you want to hear my comedy set?" says one of the guys in the golf
cart to the even emptier tent.

"Sure," someone says, and he gets up on the stage and starts his comedy set which consists of insulting everyone in the tent.

"Hey, fat-ass, you got a watermelon under that shirt?" He says to a
hefty 'lo, who in turn storms out of the tent with his ninjas, cussing
out the comic.

"Fuck you," they say.

"Yeah, you're girlfriend looks like she has hepatitis," he says to the backs of their heads.

"Look at this guy, with his glasses and his notebook," he says, pointing me out.

"He's a nerd," replies one of his homies in the cart.

"Yeah, but he's staying for my set, so he's cool."

He insults a few more in the tent. He's clearly not stopping until somebody makes him.

It comes back around to me,

"And yeah, fuck him for writing through my set."

Oddly, he doesn't say anything else as I walk out of the tent.

I walk back to the van, nauseated and wishing for a place to hide from the heat. Damon hangs out with Jared, drinking cold beer from the cooler. Jared drags off a blunt adding to the already thick air. He tells us about the time a few years ago when a carjacker jumped in his car at a red light. His first impulse was to push the gun down and away from him and it fired.

"The gun went off and shattered my leg. My leg was completely destroyed. I was housebound for three years. I mean, I could get around in a wheelchair, but it was fucking hard as hell to do. So I just went to school online and got my degree. I was able to get a scholarship because of what happened to me," he says, blowing grapey smoke into the air.

He continues to tell us about how his ex-girlfriend emptied his house of anything valuable, and his bank account of all his money while he was laid up in the hospital, but he seems to make the best of it.

I believe Juggalos like Kentucky who regard the violence in Wicked Shit as a healthy release of anger and aggression. But it doesn't always work out that way–sometimes violence manifests in worse ways than just throwing rocks and shit at a D-list celebrity. Murders happen in the name of the Hatchet. A quick Google search shows quite a few grisly crimes committed by Juggalos (and actually, I'll go ahead and say self-described Juggalos because most Juggalos dismiss them as Juffalos and I'm in no place to decide who is a real Juggalo).

Take for example the grisly case of Syko Sam. Robert McCroskey, aka Syko Sam, a twenty-old horrorcore rapper killed four people in the small town of Farmville, Virginia. First he bludgeoned his 16 year-old girlfriend, Emma Neiderbrock and her 18 year-old friend Melanie Wells to death with a hammer and a maul. Then he waited around Emma's house until her father, Pastor Marl Neiderbrock, and his estranged wife Dr. Debra Kelley came home and killed them in the same manner.

It reminds me of the disgust a writing peer and friend of mine once showed for the Juggalos, her attention drawn to them after I began talking about this project.

> "I saw a Juggalo walking with a much smaller, much younger girl. He had all that clown makeup on and they were just walking down the street. It pissed me off. I just wanted to save her."

It's not surprising to hear her say that. She's a different kind of writer than me in a lot of ways, a romantic. Her zines possess a dignified observance of beauty, even when writing about tragedies, like deaths of friends or humanity's destruction of the earth. Her voice comes from a place of the sublime.

> "They're not even human," she said of the Juggalos, only half-joking, after telling her story of seeing them on the street.

She hates what the Juggalos stand for, the Juggalos and everything about them, but mostly the violence gets to her.

> "Why are they so violent?" She asks.

For a lot of Juggalos, they were raised around violence and know it all too well. In the corners and margins of America, from the ghettos to the trailer parks, society completely stripped the underclass of culture, heritage and dignity, and with it their sense of identity. The only trait passed down to them is violence. They are born on the receiving end of this violence. Whether the violence takes the active or passive route, whether turned inward with alcoholism or meth addictions or cast back out into their environment through incest and spousal abuse, the poor know the language of violence well. Songs about whimsical rape and mutilation by clown characters add a level of play to this violence and flips it, and Juggalos are able to detach themselves from it, to abstract it, to laugh at it. When they take on clown names like Bloodshed or Stabbo or Ripper they own it through the Dark Carnival. They find room to process a very real violence through abstract satire that appears base and low-class to non-Juggalos, a sentiment which only feeds their loyalty. This violence may be hard for the outsider to understand, but for the Juggalos, it is their inheritance.

I don't beat women, fuck that/I'm above it/
but I'll cut her fucking neck and think nothing of it.
-Insane Clown Posse

"We did horrible things," Violent J says of he and Shaggy's thugging days in *Behind the Paint*, "there were these hookers who used to hang out in front of this motorcycle club called the Iron Coffins, and we'd call them over like we were going to pick them up. Right when they'd lean over into the window, we'd whip bricks at their faces like, 'bitch, get the hell out of here.' We would leave them lying bloody in the street. I can't believe we actually did that shit, now."

As sadistic as this sounds, at least Violent J refers to it as something he's moved on from. He seems repentant of it, if not regretful. For this reason alone, I find the boastful tone he takes on later, when bragging about beating the shit out of audience members more repulsive, particularly a time when a crowd-surfer flipped them off and they beat him with a mic stand to the point where he ended up in the hospital. When some

Juggalos came forward as witnesses, ICP dismissed them as fake Juggalos, just like they quickly dismiss Juggalos like Syko Sam who commit senseless murder. Beating the shit out of an audience member who throws up an insulting gesture may be less horrific than bludgeoning four people to death, but both acts require a lack of impulse control. Both acts are egocentric; Syko Sam acted to get revenge on the world and to make people submit to his will. For ICP, they act because they believe God blessed them, because they are above criticism, and they want ninjas to submit to their will. I believe ICP tends to make moral judgments according to how actions and outcomes benefit them. Being associated with Syko Sam reflects on them badly, and letting a guy get away with flipping them off wounds their ego and makes them appear weak. They responded in accordance to their beliefs in each situation

I think the title Psychopathic Records gives away more than ICP intends. They seem to take no responsibility and show little remorse for their own violence, while at the same time teaching morality, however warped, to their followers.

Even ICP's lyrics to their songs, which they claim are moral tales, elicit confusion. Plenty of victims of the Wicked Clown in the songs aren't rich or wife-beaters. They constantly flip back and forth in their justification of violence. When it's against innocents, such as a cat or a woman, they consider the violence a fantasy. When it's against kid diddlers and wife-beaters, the violence is warranted. They fall into the basic trappings of faith–by being blessed with the Dark Carnival prophecy; they seem to think they only act correctly. They fail to see their own actions and lifestyles as hypocritical to their message. I could chalk it up to male privilege, or wealth, but ICP seems to remain completely obtuse to their own actions. Psychopathic.

Damon and I sweat it out in the Freakshow Tent. Flec's Circus Sideshow performs on the stage. We just watched a guy breathe fire, a woman carry out some hula hoop tricks and a pretty impressive display of contact juggling. A guy with an "octo-bong," a beer bong with five hoses and a collapsible stand that extends several feet to accommodate the chuggers from a standing position mills about the tent. Also near us stands a white kid, his braided hair tied with multi-colored rubber bands. He couldn't be more than eighteen, but is probably somewhere closer fifteen. He wears a T-shirt that displays the saying, "Juggalo, Porch Monkey For Life" on the back, a crude misunderstanding of an already controversial joke from the movie *Clerks 2*.

Crew members unload a huge rubber ring with "Slick Chix" written on the side into the tent and machine-inflate it in just a few minutes. The MC and owner of Slick Chix starts announcing the beginning of Ladies' Oil Wrestling. He's got that short, spiky haircut with frosted tips that's popular with schmucks. My brain fails to recall his name in the heat so let's just call him Dick Macken. Dick Macken starts the event by telling everyone not to throw shit during the event or he'll shut it down. He also says cable television will air the event show later (on a station focusing on video games) and the Juggalos "WHOOP! WHOOP!" and he instructs,

> "Before we get started, I want everyone to shout with me, FUCK GIRLS GONE WILD! Say it for the camera, this is going to be on television, SAY IT LOUD FOR THE CAMERA! FUCK GIRLS GONE WILD!"

> "FUCK GIRLS GONE WILD!" The Juggalos chant as more and more of them crowd around the ring.

> "FUCK GIRLS GONE WILD!" Dick leads.

> "FUCK GIRLS GONE WILD!" The Juggalos chant back.

Eventually, some girls wearing Slick Chix swimsuits climb into the ring. Dick reminds the Juggalos he'll shut it down if they throw shit and announces the names of the two wrestlers.

> "Now,' he says, 'we come to a favorite part of the show for the Juggalos that I like to call 'Oiling Down The Bitch.'"

He grabs two teen 'los out of the audience and hands each of them a bottle of baby oil which they start spraying on the Slick Chix.

"No, no that's not how you do it,' he says, taking the bottle back, 'This is how you do it."

He spreads the girls legs apart and holds the bottle to his crotch, makes some orgasm-simulating grunts and squirts oil all over the girl. He gives the bottle back to the Juggalo who, with a hint of awkwardness, follows suit. Teenage Juggalos crowd around the wrestler smacking her ass. She smiles and writhes as the oil cascades over her, soaking her. Uncomfortable, I scan the crowd and see a Juggalo near me holding his five-year-old Juggalette daughter on his shoulders.

After a few rounds of frosted Dick's girls wrestling, he starts pulling Juggalettes from the crowd to compete. In this particular match, the first one to rip the bikini off the other Juggalette declares victory.

"Our first contestant is..." He holds the microphone to the very young 'lette.

"Tammy," she says.

"Do you have a boyfriend?" Macken asks.

"No."

"Do you want one?' He says, then seeming to forget where he is and what he's doing tells her over the mic, 'go to my website, dick-macken-dot-com. You'll see how much money I make."

Then he remembers he's announcing an event and turns to the crowd,

"Uh, you guys all check it out too dick-macken-dot-com."

The wrestler's start ripping each others clothes off and rolling in the oil. The sweaty Juggalos press tightly around the ring for a view, while the 'los behind them curve their heads up and over and side to side to get a glimpse. I join in but never get a view of the ring, and when I catch myself straining around the Juggalos for a better view, I tell Damon I've had enough. I'm hot, sticky, offended, aroused and wondering how many people I know might stumble upon a cable channel focusing on video games. I see Nathan and Samantha, the Portland couple, in the crowd as I walk from the tent. We smile at each other and shrug.

Juggalos and the LGBTQ Community

That night when I got back from my first walk in years and years, I didn't reach for those chips. I said to myself, "Those are faggot chips. For every chip I eat a homo gets to grab my balls."
-Violent J on dieting

Fuck Forrest Gump/he probably takes it in the rump
-Insane Clown Posse

"Yo, you all caressing my hand 'n' shit," Adam, a shirtless white Juggalo in HatchetGear basketball shorts says loudly, cutting his interview short by jerking his hand back from my handshake and storming off, offended. He acted really cool before that, talking about what the Family and the Dark Carnival meant to him.

"No wait...," I say, somewhat taken aback and confused.

"Nah, dog, you were caressin' my hand 'n' shit," he repeats and stomps out of Spazzmatic.

"Don't worry about him,' his homie, James, a chubby 'lo of sixteen, says, 'he's just really drunk."

James, still curious about my attempts at getting the Juggalo story, and wanting to tell his, apologizes for his friend's behavior and tries to make up for it. I keep recording and feign interest, but in my mind I try to process what just happened. Adam's problem with my "caressin'" handshake probably comes from Violent J's frequent complaining about "feeble" and "ginger-ass" handshakes. For instance, Violent J complains in his book about how all the wrestlers he's met shake hands in this wimpy way. It's a pet peeve of his. Adam appears influenced by J's alpha-male handshake predisposition enough for him to question my masculinity and sexuality (or maybe his own sexuality). Maybe I make some assumptions here. Maybe he never heard Violent J's handshake policy. Maybe he came up with it on his own. Maybe I just never noticed my extra hand-caressin' handshake and it actually exists. Whatever. My handshake clearly threatened threatened this 'los masculinity, bringing up a topic that deserves a look: does the Juggalo Family accept LGBT and queer folks? ICP shows their usual ambivalent moral flip-flopping on this matter they show with everything else. ICP, in their elevated position, influence the Juggalos of course, but how Juggalos on a ground level accept LGBT and queer people into the fold is another thing altogether. And as a subculture which claims to accept outsiders and not tolerate bigots, noting where they stand on this is crucial.

Violent J claims to have no problems with gay people, but also seems to have no problem, whatsoever, throwing around the word faggot and ICP generally regulates haters by associating them with dick sucking. Overall, ICP seems to behave genuinely intimidated by any threat to male hegemony, and it extends far beyond handshakes. But what about the Juggalo Family? I certainly heard plenty of Juggalos call each other faggot at the Gathering, but that merely shows their ignorance, and since ICP encourages ignorance, this is expected. Especially when I consider how common homophobia is in the impoverished communities a lot of the Juggalos live in. Not to mention Juggalos originated in the inherently backwards and homophobic American culture. So, for the sake of story, I'll give the Juggalos a mulligan on their on-the-surface-slurring and dig a little deeper to see how they might really feel about the LGBTQ community. It compels me, at least, because I view this acceptance as a litmus test for the validity of any culture.

To deny the misogyny and homophobia of the larger hip-hop culture (and, by proxy, its influence on ICP and Wicked Shit) would be hypocritical. Homophobia is woven into the very fiber of hip-hop. I tolerate more bigoted homophobic lyrics in rap more than other styles of music, not because I excuse it, but simply because it's so ubiquitous to the genre that one almost has to put up with it if they want to continue listening. Much of hip-hop historically relies, rather weak-mindedly, on the gender binary and regressive hyper-masculine tendencies. I could cite many reasons for this, from the fact rap rose from the streets where an outward display of "strength" coincides with survival to the possibly that rappers, DJs and graffiti writers battle for dominance in a competition-oriented subculture. Whatever the reason, a progressive hip-hop fan finds a way to justify a culture digressing to the point where many MC battles act as mere vehicles for two rappers finding fresh ways to accuse each other of being gay for three rounds.

When I bring up this point, others often counter with arguments like "that's not all hip-hop" or "that's just gangsta rap" or "that's just mainstream rap." Sure, record labels throw money at rappers who shock and stir up controversy because they sell more albums, but blaming misogyny and homophobia on a particular style of rap that isn't your cup of tea is a cop-out. And while plenty of hip-hop artists out there aren't homophobic, one questions their (and their fan's) tolerance of this bigotry When an MC disses another by calling them gay in order to imply weakness or throws out the "no homo" phrase after rapping about other MCs being on their dicks, they create a breeding ground for bigotry and closed-mindedness within the culture while further alienating and marginalizing minorities. These acts constantly reaffirm straight male hegemony. Even some "conscious" rappers fall into this, and liberal and progressive rap fans excuse the behavior (take, for instance, Mos Def, who dissed other rappers by saying, "cats who claimin' they hard be mad fag/ so I run through 'em like flood water through sandbags"). The progressive rap fans might make compromises out of jadedness to a statements ubiquity or they may not want to dismiss some of the more positive messages a rapper says. Either way, this tolerance comes from a lack of shock at the genre's understated fear and hatred of LGBTQ people and subjugation of anything associated with the feminine. This sets a precedent that has festered in rap to the point where unapologetic bigots can violently target LGBT and queer-identifying folks with little reprisal. Such as the well-respected MC of Jedi Mind Tricks' Vinnie Paz, who spits vile and fascist lyrics like "listen I ain't gonna play no more, beat a faggot 'til he ain't fucking gay no more" that no longer just degrade, but actually target gay folks.

Fortunately, more and more music journalists, bloggers and rappers themselves (like Kanye West and Snoop Dogg, who both came out in defense of the LGBT community) address and deconstruct these important topics. What's important here is seeing how the bigotry and misogyny of hip-hop culture influenced the Juggalo Family. Since Wicked Shit exists as an offshoot of rap, the music echoes some of larger hip-hop's knuckle-dragging vernacular, but how does it translate to the Juggalo Family, a group that claims to accept outsiders?

My pre-Gathering research revealed little. Looking up "gay + Juggalo" only revealed Juggalos and non-Juggalos insulting each other on internet forums. Save for a few bisexual male Juggalos on Juggalo dating sites (yes, they have them), I found little. The existence of J-FLAG (Juggalo Family of Lesbians and Gays) impressed me but they appear inactive. It seemed the Gathering was the only place I'd get the scoop.

"No, I don't have a problem with gay people," Kentucky enthusiastically tells me, "if that's what you're into then that's fine."

Most Juggalos I talk to share the same attitude when asked, but that only includes Juggalos I actually talk to. I don't talk to Juggalos who throw trash all day and chant for titties. But then again, a lot of those Juggalos are close to high school age. My friends and I were also loose with those words in high school, and if what I hear on the street is any indication, most teenage boys still call each other faggot. My short conversations with Juggalos of the more close-minded sort end poorly, often with me moving along out of fear of catching a beatdown (for not being a Juggalo) or them moving along out of fear of a fey handshake.

"If you're Fam, you're Fam," Juggalos who allow me to broach the topic repeatedly answer. Nonetheless, I get the impression they spend little time thinking about it at all, as if they've never really been faced with it. That said, they seem to care little about who their Family fucks. In this way, the Juggalo Family transcends the less-than-progressive backgrounds most of them come from. In spite of the numerous Wicked Shit songs referring to butt fucking and dick sucking as weak acts, when it comes to tribalism and community many Juggalos seem to care for their own enough to show respect.

I can't deny the obvious, though, there aren't a lot of out queer people here at all, which makes sense. Sid, the one out queer person I meet here views his treatment in the Family positively. He's a transman who totally gets down with the Clown.

"I feel accepted here, 'cause it's really not no big thing," Sid says; he identifies in the Family as lesbian but not always as trans, "as a trans person, though...'Cause I am trans, as well..Female to male. I don't know. I don't really tell too many people that shit. Normally, I'll just tell people that I prefer male pronouns or to just call me by my name and that's usually what they do. I've had, like, a couple homies back where I live who are like, 'you have tits, you're a chick' and that's fucked up, but it's because of how you were taught and whatever, how you were raised. It's got nothing to do with being a Juggalo, like they still accept me as Family and shit. But, you know, they step on my toes with that shit, but whatever. And here, ya know, the only thing that really pisses me off is just hearing "fag" all the time but that's everywhere. And it's just like, it sucks, but whatever. I've heard about two gay Juggalos holding hands by the lake. So it's here."

Sid also retells a rumor he heard about Shaggy and Violent J intervening to break up a gay-bashing at one of their shows. When he brings up this evidence in this manner I assume he thought about it quite a bit. Like he tries to find stuff to help alleviate his alienation at not having fellow queer folks in the Juggalo Family, but he still feels comfortable and accepted, at least enough to stick around. He loves the Fam because he "came out with only ten bucks in his pocket," but the Juggalos took care of him, giving him all the food and weed he couldn't afford. As he talks to me about his experiences as trans and in the Family, a few other Juggalos Sid hangs out with nod approval and back him up.

"Yeah...I don't feel like, 'hell, yeah! I can come out here with my packet and shit and, like, be a big trans dyke and shit', 'cause people will probably be like 'uhh...what the fuck?' I'm not a big fan of that, but I also feel like if I were to do that they wouldn't care too much, either. It's just be, like, to each his own. Shit, it's not shit, you know, like you wanna be a trans dyke or whatever, do your thing," Sid says.

"Yeah, just do your thing. That's a perfect way to put it," Topher agrees.

I never get to the bottom of it out here since I simply cannot talk to every Juggalo at the Gathering, nor do I sit down and deconstruct the lyrics to homophobic ICP songs with Juggalos. I don't get the chance ask every Juggalo why they flip toss around faggot as an insult. I certainly am not able to get into in any complex discussions of sexuality. Also, most of the Juggalos I meet try to prove to me the open-minded awesomeness of their Family, which skews the information I collect. Simply speaking to the Juggalos who willingly talk to me, however faulty a control group, many express the same sentiment as Sid and Topher–just do your thing.

Twiztid Seminar

No more knocking on the door
We moshing on the floor and shit
And we ain't leaving till we heaving up some blood and shit
Fuck a mother fucking Twix, bitch
I'd rather roll with the clique of lunatics
That's now known as TWIZTID!!
-Monoxide Child of Twiztid

A few thousand bodies once again cram into the stifling heat of the Seminar Tent, this time to participate in the Twiztid seminar. Loud shop fans blow from the stage onto the crowd but offer little relief. The heat causes us to swelter so much most of the 'los give up on the face paint. One Juggalo, a thin guy in his early twenties with short cropped hair, holds tight, sweating through his make-up. Beads of sweat cascade down the pasty white and glaring green of his clown face, but his hand resists reaching to wipe it. He just stares at the empty stage intently. He wears the more gothic Juggalo look (as opposed to the usual baggy clothes aesthetic) wearing tight, black pants tucked into tall platform boots with lots of straps that stop just above the knee. I'm nauseated and groggy from the heat but still feel a twinge of pity for how much more uncomfortable he must be. I see him around the Gathering frequently, and though I haven't approached him, everything about him screams true believer.

A huge "WHOOP! WHOOP!" rises up from the crowd as Twiztid struts on to the stage. They wear matching oversized T-shirts with red and black gothic lettering and a picture of an eagle with spread wings. Monoxide Child, the skinnier one, wears a red ball cap backwards and tilted to the side. Jamie Madrox, the self-proclaimed fat one, wears three small braids on the top of his head in a line. Neither of them wear make-up. I can't tell from where I stand whether or not they wear their evil contacts.

"What up, y'all?" Monoxide addresses the crowd. "It's a lot cooler in here," he says referring to the fans blowing behind them on stage, "How are ya?"

The Juggalos answer back in a torrent of shouting and WHOOP! WHOOP!ing.

"Did someone get stabbed? Was I misinformed?" Monoxide asks the crowd with a smile.

Another huge, "WHOOP! WHOOP!"comes up from the crowd. Aside from the Tila attack, the only other notable assault at the Gathering was between two carnies fighting over backstage passes, which ended in a stabbing, or so the rumor goes. After addressing the stabbing, Madrox and Monoxide start riffing, beginning with the weather. Madrox, the fat one, proposes a winter Gathering, and a the audience yells a huge WHOOP! WHOOP!

"I'll have you know, I'm gonna start pre-selling tickets to my winter Gathering," he says in a ragged and croaking voice and gets the 'los WHOOP! WHOOP!ing again.

"As it sits, I have six tickets sold,' he continues, 'so that means there's six fat kids here that would love to have Faygo snowball Armageddon…"

"WHOOP! WHOOP!"

"The Snow Boot Running Challenge…"

"WHOOP! WHOOP!"

"The Who-Put-The-Dick-On-The-Snowman Challenge…"

"WHOOP! WHOOP!"

"Here's what I see," Monoxide interrupts, "me on stage…urine-soaked snowballs…" He says and feigns a Juggalo lobbing one at him, and continues, "I'm gonna poop in this one," feigning another throw.

The Juggalos laugh loudly.

"If one of y'all threw a diarrhea ball at me, we wouldn't be friends no more. I'd just have to cut the relationship off. But, man, if I got hit with feces, I thought it was all love."

The Juggalos laugh more.

"This year the love was strong. I got hit with one of everything in this bitch. Beer cans. Bottles of pop. Someone threw an RV sink at me. What up, Fam?" Monoxide declares.

"I want to know who the Keystone Bandit is, the guy who's got the shittiest beer in the world. They like grip 'em like fucking grenades" he says imitating pulling out the pin and throwing one, "and they scope people. This guy has accuracy. No matter where you are he will scope you out and get your motherfuckin' ass."

The Juggalos just keep cracking up and WHOOP! WHOOP!ing.

They segue back into Madrox joking about the heat, about how he "saw ninjas on the side of the road with heatstroke and people looking all lifeless and dead like an Alice In Chains song."

"We spent two whole nights riding around the campground just to make sure that people weren't dead," Monoxide says.

"Passing out little Dixie cups of water," Madrox continues.

"Giving them a little pat on the balls," adds Monoxide.

The Juggalos laugh hysterically.

"Here drink this Dixie Cup. Stay hydrated. Like, I could piss more than a Dixie Cup," pronounces Madrox.

"That'll be three dollars," says Monoxide.

"Right. How are you gonna charge three dollars for a Dixie Cup of water?" Madrox asks.

"A motherfucker tried to sell me a sandwich bag full of dirt and grass, saying, 'I got Gathering crops for four bucks!'" Monoxide claims.

"Oh, c'mon, it's like pieces of the Berlin Wall. This is official Lake Hepatitis water and you know how it's official 'cause of the rubber band on the top and not like the rubber band you put around your money, it's the cock rubber band from the rubber,' exclaims Madrox, making a toss-off motion in front of his crotch. 'That's how you know it's official, and I know some of y'all still got your towels still on. I'm a let you know, we done told you y'all every year, Lake Hepatitis is a no-go for the Juggalo," he continues amid more laughter from the Juggalos.

"But I can't front, for some of them motherfuckers, it's either Lake Hepatitis or die," Monoxide says, throwing a bone to the audience, because after all, the lake offers the only escape from the heat.

"Fair enough," Madrox banters back, "but, OK, here's the condom and you're swimming," he flails his arms imitating a Juggalo frog-stroking the condom away from him, "trying to get away from it and its got a little milk in it. I know that ain't frosting because I ain't had no Pop Tart."

The Juggalos convulse and reel with laughter, shaking and folding over in the heat. It almost seems rehearsed, the way Jamie and Madrox volley off of each other. One bounces around behind the other with sound affects and pantomimes of what the other describes. Moving from one topic to the next, sometimes rehashing a previous crowd favorite (like the Lake Hepatitis condom) and the Family roars with approval. They act like of a bunch of high school or college friends sitting around a particle board coffee table, bloated with beer spillage, passing a bong in their first apartment, trying to outdo each other in gross-out jokes. But Twiztid ties the crowd around their finger.

Madrox excitedly retells a story about when they found Star Trek cereal at a store in a town near here.

"We were all hype. We had our milk. We sat down with our bowls. We looked at the expiration date and that bitch was from two years ago."

"Stardate, 1987, captain's log," Monoxide dramatically announces.

"We ate the shit. It was super nasty, but we ate the shit. We were going to bring the rest out and throw it out like duck feed and just see who wanted to catch it. Mite, mite, mite,' Madrox imitates a duck quacking, 'sprinklin' y'all with marshmallows and l'il cinnabons 'n' shit."

This leads into a debate over Star Trek and Star Wars. They consider themselves fans of both, but Monoxide prefers Star Wars and Madrox prefers Star Trek. Madrox's choice elicits some boos from the Juggalos.

"When it goes down,' Madrox disses Luke Skywalker, 'he's riding in a broke down Landspeeder with two droids and Captain Kirk's up there fucking some green bitch, like, yeah," He goes on saying Captain Kirk taught him everything he knows about sex.

"I'm like, let me beam you up! Let me beam you up," he says thrusting his crotch, while Monoxide mimics the theme song into the microphone.

After some time, someone in their crew finds the Star Trek Cereal and passes it to the stage. Madrox gets his wish and walks across the front of the stage, emptying the box into the open hands and mouths of the Juggalos.

"Mite, mite, mite," he says.

They start taking questions from the audience. A Juggalette gets up and asks if she can get her bong signed and a hug from Madrox. They agree to sign the bong, but not to the hug. Most of the Juggalos asking for autographs claim they stood in line for hours but the autograph session still ended before they could get theirs. They sign a few, but then cut it off. Otherwise, that's all they'd do.

"You better not ask for an autograph," he says to a 'lette in the crowd, but it's not an autograph she wants.

"Can I have a hug from you guys?" She asks.

They turn her down but other 'lettes keep trying. The Juggalettes flirt with Twiztid, the sex stars of the Psychopathic Family, especially the hefty Madrox, an unconventional heartthrob. The Juggalettes seem to flock to them because of their psychosexual lyrics.

> "Heyyy, Jamie and Paul (Monoxide's first name)," a young, thin 'lette says addressing them in an overly sensuous flirty falsetto.

> "Heyyy," they tease her in unison.

> "I was wondering. I know you all rhyme about some crazy sexual shit you do. Well, what's the craziest freakiest sexual shit you've ever done?"

> "You got about two hours, I'll tell you some shit," Monoxide says.

> "That's like some personal intimate shit and if we tell it and we get intimate with some bitch, she'll be like all he did was just have sex with me. He didn't piss in my ear like he said he would on stage. He didn't rub his ass cheek on my titty. You're gonna steal all my Jedi Secrets, I can't tell those."

When a Juggalo brings up Tila Tequila, Monoxide says,

> "We ain't going to talk about that, because we all see it a different way. There's no sense in creating a line."

A Juggalo from the crowd with a stoned-sounding voice says he bought a jersey from his friend who claimed there were only ever two made. He asks Twiztid to verify the legitimacy of the statement.

> "Oh, for real," Madrox says, "you want that approved. No, there was more than two of those made. They lied to you," but then tells him it's still dope and not a bootleg.

I don't know why, but I keep hoping for a 'lo to question why they only played half a set. Part of me wants to think at least one Juggalo felt he got a raw deal after coming this far.

One Juggalo gets up and says,

> "After your abbreviated set last night, I heard a couple people talking some shit on the new album and I want to say 'fuck that,' that shit was hot. I loved it."

They thank him and say the Juggalos can think whatever they want, but Twiztid still put together the album for them. They made it as gift and aren't mad if the 'los don't like it.

> "Last year, didn't you say that you were going to bring something special to the Gathering?" a Juggalo asks.

> "We did, it was a record. It's the most special thing we could think of next to our children. Right now, that's the thing that means the absolute most to us and to share it with y'all, it was the shit," Monoxide responds.

The next girl in line says she intended to ask her question to ICP, but the seminar ended before she got a chance to ask. Then she asks about the importance of the Number 17, a number crucial to ICP mythology, and a sort of legendary nod to the mere 17 copies sold on the release day of ICP's first album. The number also has a lot of synchronicity with Violent J and Shaggy, which they apply to the Dark Carnival. The question is long, meandering and hard to follow, so Monoxide cuts her off,

> "Do your research on ICP and the Number 17. It will explain it all. Thank you for coming. Sit back down."

> "It looks like her first Gathering, we were all Gathering virgins at one time," Madrox says playfully to the rest of the Family. "I'm just saying, for everyone who's ready to Tila Tequila her," his tone gets real.

> "Let me explain something to you. This is what I've learned,' Monoxide says, 'There's two sets of Juggalos. There's the motherfuckers who wear the paint all the time and just live the shit, right? I mean fuckin' live it"

The platform-booted Juggalo nods somberly through his green painted-on grin. Monoxide goes on,

"and then there's the other who just...casually...They like it. They dig the music they dig the atmosphere. They don't necessarily paint up but they'll come out to the shows, buy your merch or whatever. The crazy thing is y'all can't get along. What I don't understand is where the separation came between y'all; that shit is insane to me. I don't know where the message got twisted. It's a whole other seminar, but it's something to think about. I want to know what makes these Juggalos so much better than these Juggalos. I want to hear it for real, 'cause I'm baffled by the shit."

The Juggalos grow quiet and listen intently for a moment, leaving out the cheering and WHOOP! WHOOP!ing.

"If it's real Family love, than look out for your motherfuckin' Family. Or we need to make up a new word and quit frontin'," he continues.

"DISTANT COUSIN! DISTANT COUSIN!' Madrox chants into the mic, 'cause that's what it's like. You see a motherfucker layin', pukin' in the shit and everybody like 'let's go kick 'em'. If that's your Family, help that motherfucker out. Set him up. Get him an ice cold water. Show the Love."

"'I'll tell you a hundred percent, a Juggalo is a Juggalo,' Madrox says, 'to bomb on somebody because they're not as hard-core as you is wack."

"That's why we come out with no paint on, so the shock will wear off. So y'all will understand," Monoxide explains.

The Juggalos quietly listen, mesmerized.

"We're just like you. There's nothing different between me and you but the microphone and we speak for you so you should respect that,' Madrox declares, 'if you want to leave here and kick a Juggalo and then go home and think about it, that's fine. I'm not tellin' ya what to do. I'm not your daddy. I'm your brother. And if we love each other we can grow as a Family and not as a cult. Not as a bunch of mindless fuckers who don't know. Respect the motherfucker next to you. Respect the bitch next to you."

The Juggalos "WHOOP! WHOOP!" Loudly in agreement. Then time runs out. The seminar ends.

Breaking Down Camp

Ain't nobody jealous, everybody has they own
Nobody locked up, everybody, everybody is free to roam
Lookin' at scrubby with a hottie on his side
Lookin' at rich kids, poor kids,
Everybody together on the same side
And they down to ride
-Insane Clown Posse

"I let you guys run shit for a while. Now I gotta get mine," says a Black guy in a Chicago Bulls basketball jersey to a small, dirty, long-haired kid.

The kid holds a sign written on 12-pack cardboard, "Rolls $15.00, $10.00, $7.00, $5.00." In Chicago's outward palm lays a packet of colorful blue pills, presumably of a higher quality.

"I'm just trying to get home," the kid says.

So much trash litters the ground, at this point, that in some places, it equals the amount of visible earth. We just kick through it as we walk and duck when it flies through the air. The Juggalos are stoked ICP takes the stage in a few hours. But melancholy permeates the air as everyone breaks down their camps, packing up the physical manifestation of the Dark Carnival, leaving their hearts to carry it on until next Gathering.

Everyone spent all of their money, and are left hustling anything and everything for gas money. A few drugs remain for sale on Drug Bridge, but they've mostly been replaced with a lot more of everything else. You can get as many Jell-O shots as you can carry for $5 bucks. Packs of cigarettes get dumped into piles, sold for fifty cents apiece. Swigs of whiskey or vodka go for whatever one can throw down. Apparently, titty-flashes still work as currency and near me a couple smoke bombs go off.

"Hey ninja, are you writing?" A Juggalo asks me on Drug Bridge, breaking me out of the spell of writing all of this down in my small black journal.

"Oh...yeah..." I say.

"I was just asking because, I've never seen anybody writing here before. What are you writing about?"

"Oh, just all of this, you know, what I'm experiencing."

"That's cool," he says.

I pull out my camera to take a few pictures.

"Hey, what kind of camera is that," a big Juggalo asks me as he walks by with a group of four other pretty big dudes.

"Um, a Nikon," I stammer, not sure what to say

"A Nikon,' his buddy mocks, 'it's a Nikon," his tone vaguely threatening.

I'm not sure where this is going, but I'm starting to wonder if I wore out my welcome. I wonder if I said too much about my purpose when blacked out at some point. I put my camera back in my bag and head back to the van.

The clouds move in as Damon and I pass our last fifth back and forth, sitting in the van with the side door open. The impending rain thickens the air, different from the thick hot humidity that permeated the Gathering over the last four days. We hand our fifth off to whoever moseys by the van. Some we know well by now, while others we just meet as they pass through. It reminds me of the old days, Damon and I, somewhere we don't belong, acting like a couple of dumbasses and laughing a lot, nearing the end of our adventure

"Aw, man, it looks like it's that time," I tell Damon, and get up to take a shit.

We both avoided the mortifying port-a-potties, prolonging the inevitable by packing ourselves with nothing but summer sausage and cheese.

"Get a clean break," he advises.

I refuse to use the port-a-potties, and choose to shit in the woods instead. I grab a roll of toilet paper and head off the property, under a barbed wire fence, past a cop parked off property in an Explorer guarding the road. I turn to head down into a ravine when I find a carpet of poison ivy. I think again of the state of the port-a-potties, cross my fingers, hoping I still possess the immunity to poison ivy I had as a kid, and plow right through it to climb down the ravine. I find a dry gully, squat down and do my business.

As I scramble through the brush to get out, the sprinkling starts. Down comes the heavy, cold, Midwestern rain of my youth. The sky dumps the redemptive, heavy torrents I left behind long ago for Seattle's steady drizzle. The rain soaks my clothes, mud clings to the fabric, and I shiver and smile. I'm far away from all of the trash and merchandise, and aside for a few RVs and trailers, I'm isolated. I walk back, drunk on whiskey and gaze up through my spotted glasses into the pouring shower. The thick film of Hepatitis Lake washes away, along with my own sweat and the grime of Hogrock. I head back to the van and sit on the bumper, getting soaked in the downpour.

The shower ends and kicks a glorious lavender sunset across the sky.

"Check that out,' I say to a Juggalette parked near us, 'fucking amazing."

"What..?" She asks, and then she sees me pointing.

"The sunset," I say.

"Oh...yeah...," she says.

I notice she's changing between two cars into an outfit to wear to ICP's show tonight. I realize she might have thought I referred to her in her half-dressed state, and thus thought she was being leered at yet again.

But maybe the sunset just didn't impress her, most likely, probably a bit of both fueled her hesitation. I continue to watch the sun go down, cooled off and renewed. Living in Seattle with the misty drizzle, I often miss the heavy rain and thunderstorms of the Midwest and the South, the comforting ambiance of a downpour and the funny feeling I get in my stomach and spine when I hear the thunder crack and roll. Soon, the insular bubble nature holds me in bursts by a couple of cars pulling away from the campsite.

"What the fuck?" A Juggalo in full face-paint exclaims, throwing his arms up in confused frustration,"they're leaving before ICP! Why the fuck would you do that, 'lo? That's fucked up"

"I don't know, ninja," I say and shrug, jarred out of my spell.

"Hey, has Spice 1 played yet?" I ask him, remembering where I am.

It turns out that Spice 1, an old school gangsta rap MC canceled, along with Slick Rick, so I miss another act I hoped to see. ICP often relays how hard it is to get acts to play the Gathering, and how a lot of them back out at the last minute (particularly ones I want to see). Damon wakes up, comes up over my shoulder and hands me the whiskey bottle.

"Time to live the chaos," he says, grinning.

I wash down the last of the Vicodan we scored the night before and we head to the main stage.

We run into Nathan and Samantha on the way to the main stage. A white garbage bag filled with beer hangs over Nathan's shoulder and a thick layer of white greasepaint covers his face. Samantha is dressed in her usual style.

"Hey. How's it goin'?' I ask, 'You look prepared."

"Hey, what's up?" Nathan says, his features still readable beneath the paint. "Man, I'm stoked to see ICP. I know the Juggalos can be a bit ridiculous, but ICP is still the best live band that I've ever seen."

He still wears his fitted indie-rocker-looking T-shirt but blends in just the same. We follow them towards the stage, lose them in the crowd and wait for Method Man and Redman.

"What up, Illinois?" Meth shouts to the crowd between songs.

Damon and I give each other a look that reads "Shit, no one here is from Illinois."

The forgiving audience shouts out "WHOOP! WHOOP!"

I'm super stoked to see Method Man, to the point I'd see the show any-where. Method Man may not be considered the best rapper in Wu-Tang Clan, but I always thought him my favorite. I appreciate the apocalyptic nature of his solo albums and overall aesthetic.

"How many of y'all smokin' some shit, tonight?" Meth shouts to the crowd who return with a "WHOOP! WHOOP!"

They then go into a familiar Wu-Tang hit,

"Hey you, get off my cloud, you don't know me and you don't know my style."

And another "WHOOP! WHOOP!" rises from the crowd. Wicked Shit or not, most of the Juggalos know the song.

"I got fat bags of sku-unk, I got White Owl blu-unts..." Meth and Redman throw out the call and hold the mic out to the audience.

"And I'm about to go get lifted...about to go get lifted." the 'los and I shout back.

"I've got myself a forty and I've got myself a shorty and..."

"I'm about to go and stick it...about to go and stick it."

A few bottles fly at the stage, streaks of water flash in the stage lights. The song ends to a cheer and even more "WHOOP! WHOOPS!"

"What up, Illinois?" Redman says, again throwing his arm back and forth rhythmically.

The Juggalos start chanting "FAM-UH-LEE! FAM-UH-LEE!" as Meth and Redman go into the next song.

"That bottle almost hit me, yo. Don't be throwin' shit." Meth shouts out to the audience.

Next song. Some random shit hits the stage but most of the Juggalos just have a great time shouting the choruses and throwing their arms in the air.

"FAM-UH-LEE! FAM-UH-LEE!" Go the Juggalos.

Communication breaks down between Meth and Redman and the Juggalos. Meth seems obtuse to his audience or location. Redman speaks into his ear between songs, explaining something we can't hear. They move into another song. At the end of it the crowd cheers and then,

"FAM-UH-LEE! FAM-UH-LEE!"

"What?" Meth asks the crowd.

"FAM-UH-LEE! FAM-UH-LEE!"

Redman walks over to him and says something. I notice a few random middle fingers fly up from the crowd, but most of the 'los still get down.

"FAM-UH-LEE! FAM-UH-LEE!"

"What?" Meth asks.

"FAM-UH-LEE! FAM-UH-LEE! FAM-UH-LEE!"

"What? Family? Fuck family! This is about hip-hop!"

A split forms between the crowd. Some of the 'los continue to get into the show but more and more middle fingers rise up, and all the Juggalos unite in the chant "FAM-UH-LEE!" as Meth and Redman go into their next song. Trash flies towards the stage as the DJ cuts the record short.

"Man, that shit almost hit me, that's fucked up. Stop throwing shit and we'll go on with the show."

"FAM-UH-LEE! FAM-UH-LEE! FAM-UH-LEE!"

Then, in the middle of a song, a full glass bottle flies from the crowd and hits Meth in the face. Foam flies out everywhere as it hits him. He throws down the mic angrily.

"FUCK THE NIGGA WHO THREW THAT!" Shouts Meth.

"FUCK THAT SHIT! FUCK THAT SHIT! FUCK THAT SHIT!" Chants the majority of the Juggalos, pissed off at whoever threw it.

"Yo, your face is cut,' Redman says, 'you need to get that looked at."

"FUCK THAT! I DON'T NEED THIS SHIT, MAN!" he says, "MY HEART DON'T PUMP KOOL-AID!"

"You need to get that checked out," Redman says into the mic.

"FUCK THAT! START THE MUSIC! WE'RE FINISHING THE SHOW!" Meth says.

The DJ spins the record and starts the next song.

Blood pours down his face, he wipes it off with a towel throughout the rest of the set. They finish their set to a loud chanting of "FAM-UH-LEE!" Throughout the crowd, middle fingers pop up here and there.

"FUCK Y'ALL, I DON'T PUMP KOOL-AID!" he repeats after the last song and they walk off the stage, ending the most genuinely bad-ass performance I've ever seen.

I heard rumors some of the 'los had it out for Method Man even before he said "fuck family" because of his mainstream success. I'm shocked that

Method Man and Redman made it all the way out here without having a clue where they were or who their audience was. Didn't their P.R. people or managment fill them in on the Juggalos? Did they assume the Gathering was a music festival like any other? Who knows, maybe they smoked too much before the show. Wu-Tang Clan is one of the most classic and well-respected hip-hop crews. They're famous because they changed the game, not because they played pop, and they're some of the hardest and dopest rappers ever. They're O.G.* I can't imagine why anybody would fuck with one of them. Don't fuck with a Juggalo.

Next up: ICP.

"FAM-UH-LEE! FAM-UH-LEE! FAM-UH-LEE! FAM-UH-LEE! FAM-UH-LEE! FAM-UH-LEE!"

The Juggalo's chant to a dark stage before ICP's set. I take a swill off my whiskey, the Vicodan warm and fuzzy in my stomach. Then..."BANG! POW! BOOM!" and a fifty foot set of lights wash the crowd. A blinking Hatchetman lights up on stage, followed by a blazing I, followed by a C, and then a P.

Finally "ICP" blazes in full glory with the Hatchetman right beside it, blinking on and off.

"DO YOU KNOW WHO YOU'RE FUCKING WITH?" A looped sample pounds the audience, and a heavy metal guitar riff backs the shouted, "W-W-W-W-W-W-W-WICKED! WICKED CLOWN!," followed by a sampled gun blast. "KA-POW!"

Violent J and Shaggy hit the stage all painted up and chuck two-liters of Faygo into the crowd. A thundering, "WHOOP! WHOOP!" comes up in unison from the crowd of ninjas. A warm chill runs up my spine.

"My father was a priest cold-blooded he's dead, Hypocrite, he was a bigot so I cut off his head, Poured out the holy water 'bless the dead'

*O.G is short for Original Gangsta

is what I said, And heard the demons screamin' as his body bled," Insane Clown Posse raps.

"W-W-W-W-W-W-W-WICKED CLOWN! W-W-W-W-W-W-W-WICKED CLOWN! DON'T FUCK WITH ME!"

"...hey babe, why don't ya chill and kill this two-liter, went into my trailer, I filled up the glass, before she took a sip I had my dick in her ass...," goes the rhyme.

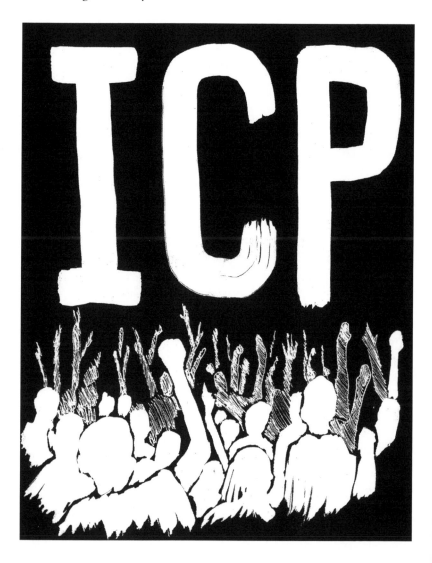

Clowns, monsters, demons, dance around Violent J and Shaggy, soaking the Family down with Faygo. The bass throbs, looped by a DJ spinning records behind a protective clear plastic sneeze guard. He throws his hands in the air and bounces between the two turntables. I put camera away and taste the salty, sugary citrus liquid running down my face as a big, fat clown with a rainbow wig and a puffy red nose wets down the 'los with a fire hose of Red Mist. Violent J and Shaggy go into number after number.

"If I only could, I'd set the world on fire. Say FUCK THE WORLD! FUCK THE WORLD!"

"FUCK THE WORLD! FUCK THE WORLD!" The crowd shouts back.

Shaggy and Violent J clutch their cordless mics in one hand and rap, while shaking up 2-liter bottles of Faygo in the other; they loosen the caps and douse the open-mouthed Juggalos. Titties get soaked and groped as Juggalettes gleefully writhe in the spray. Violent J starts drop-kicking bottle after bottle of the sticky generic soda into the crowd. Grinning rubber-masked clowns in baggy, red and yellow jumpsuits refresh the supply with crate after crate of Faygo.

"FUCK THE WORLD! FUCK THE WORLD!" ICP and the Juggalos chant.

Bottles fly through the air non-stop and the Juggalos lose their fucking minds. They hug and pass blunts while shouting out the choruses. Beach balls bounce all throughout the crowd, tight fists pound them away from wherever they land. On both sides of me, Juggalo couples embrace, kissing deeply in the cloying mist.. This is it! The moment they live for and the crowd pulsates with life, moving in waves as one giant unit. Someone passes me a joint. I hit it. WHOOP! WHOOP! Everybody rolling on E, tripping on acid or mushrooms, blunted as fuck or in a drunken stupor. The thick air sparks with unity.

"FAM-UH-LEE! FAM-UH-LEE! FAM-UH-LEE!" The crowd chants as a song fades..."FAM-UH-LEE! FAM-UH-LEE!" This quiets, and all around individual scattered "WHOOP! WHOOPS!" sporadically arise throughout the crowd, but mostly a sort of hush fills the air. And I get another chill...

I hear a tinkling piano, the beginning of a song I know. ICP begins their power ballad, If I Were A Serial Killer. Violent J's voice breaks in, poignantly singing,

> "If I Were a Serial Killer, they'd find my victims heads in funky gas station toilets" The crowd sings along, "and if I was a Serial Killer, I would be strange and deranged. And I would never change."

The emotion of the crowd crackles, understated by the calm tension of the ballad. Some lighters go up in the air. The Faygo slows to a cascade instead of the shaken-up propulsion of the heavier songs.

> "If I was a Serial Killer, I'd be known as The Smoker, 'cause I'd cut off and smoke all they hair and if I was a Serial Killer I would sleep on broken glass and thumbtacks and I would smoke mad crack," ICP and the Family sings, providing a somewhat perverted tender moment in the concert.

Hands and lighters wave back and forth in the air. The stage goes dark for a minute as a piano loop plays out the end of the song.

Then a heavy beats kicks off and the giant, blinking I...C...P lights once again flood the audience with dizzying light.

"WHOOP! WHOOP!" Go the Juggalos.

The Hatchetman sign comes back on, pulsing and pounding. The evil clowns and demons come dancing back out to join Violent J and Shaggy 2 Dope, along with a few elite chubby 'los and 'lettes slipping and sliding on the stage, spraying more Faygo onto the audience.

My head struggles to make sense of everything. The warm, buzzy, twist of whiskey, Vicodan and Clown Love still fill my body, but something fights its way through to the front of my mind. Fighting it's way through the oneness of the crowd, and I try to catch hold of it, but I lose it. I think about all the songs that filled my ears this evening, remembering all of them from my years of worthless scrutiny, and how goddamned stupid I found them. The Faygo soda combines with the dust in the air and a thick, grimy film covers my body; it may be disgusting but this is the best show I've ever seen. It embodies the Dark Carnival–it's rapturous, godlike, and as near holy as anything I saw or felt in the Pentecostal church growing up. It reminds me of God's flock flailing about the church, shouting out in tongues and falling straight to the floor, slain in the spirit after the pastor firmly pressed his palm to their forehead. I bat a beach ball away from me. Generous, offering hands hold more joints out to me. I take long drags off of them. I pass my whiskey around, and the Juggalos take it, grins plastered on their faces, their eyes turning back to the stage as they swig from the bottle.

I move to a safer distance, out of the spray, to take it all in. This is what it's all about, I think. Pure carbonated shock and awe. Faygo soaks the crowd and they work themselves into a frenzy of devotion and Wicked Clown Love. Nothing but Clown Love. At least thirty people bounce around the stage, still shaking and spraying and chucking two-liters of Faygo into the crowd. I lick the citrusy corn syrup from upper lip. My hair is soaked and ratted, my hand catches when I push it from my face. It's impossible to deny sheer power of this concert, the clown faces of Violent J and Shaggy, the wicked mask continually worn representing all of the love and humanity the 'los might ever witness.

I wipe Rock & Rye Faygo from of my eyes and stare deep into ICP's faces, eyes glassy and awash in Faygo and Clown Love. ICP's sophomoric, scatological rhymes blend together. I realize I was off track looking for answers in ICP lyrics to explain this culture. I move towards the stage as torrents of Faygo pour down on me, my gaze fixed on the faces of Insane Clown Posse. The Juggalos don't take notice of me or the spell that I'm in. I stare into the clown masks. I get it now. This is why someone becomes a Juggalo. I take a slug on my bottle of whiskey, and realize in this moment I may be the only one of these 20,000 people not experiencing complete bliss. I fixate on Violent J's clown face as he moves about the stage and feel my shirt collar stick to my neck.

"WHOOP! WHOOP!" The crowd cries out.

I watch Shaggy's mouth move but fail to hear the stage banter coming out of it. All of my obsessively trying to figure this odd subculture boils down to this one loud and charismatic concert. Is this what makes a "Juggalo for life"? And these two clowns...I keep staring into their faces, and I suspect they begin to mock me with their leering painted-on smiles, and I only see two very lucky charismatic leaders. Prophets. Pimps. The Wicked Clown's face hiding a couple of willfully ignorant, possibly psychopathic rappers from the slums of Detroit. Too hateful or fearful of knowledge to learn how magnets work, but with a single-minded expertise at sales and promotion, at processing their own greed. I see the Wicked Clown who came to Violent J in a dream in order to teach the path to Shangri-la. As I soak in a communion of Faygo and the incense of blunts, and I'm getting hit with a full force blow of what's going on and I no longer find it funny or compelling or fascinating. Even though ICP performs one hell of a show. The narcotics in my system no longer fight my analytical mind and my irritation progresses. My skin becomes itchy, pores feel clogged with fructose, and I lose my ability to just go with the flow. My false euphoria wanes; I no longer feel the Juggalo Family's unity or even the warmth and rush of a great concert. The Family love heartbeat throbs all around me but I stand still, staring into that clown face, forcing myself on this final night to process everything and everything suddenly comes into focus.

It's just one more fucking thing...one more thing for the poor and wretched of the earth to latch onto as an outlet for their rage at their poverty, their powerlessness. It acts as another distraction for the outcast, for the poor, for the downtrodden, I think as I stare into the faces of the clowns on the stage. I look at J's grinning face. I don't see the benevolence the Juggalo's claim hides beneath the wicked facade. And I know underneath all the greasepaint the Clown laughs at the floobs and scrubs who follow them. Clown Love detaches from Insane Clown Posse as I stare into that grin. It was the Juggalos who made Clown Love what it is and they did it themselves. They created a family to take care of each other, and defend each other. And me, this scrubby ex-punk rock kid trying to be a journalist, stares into the Clown face and I see it's not about the size of ones bank account, but about the size of ones heart. And Juggalos got heart. They really got fucking heart. But I see no heart in the clown faces of Violent J and Shaggy, I just see greed and lust for power excused by the all too familiar tenants of prophecy and faith.

Faith. This former tongue-speaking Pentecostal kid, sees it, in the bene-
diction on the stage. It's all too familiar. It ripples up my own spine, triggered by the crowd and fueled by Vicodan and booze. I recall my own
mother feeling the wings of an angel caress her as she thrashes about the
church, speaking in tongues when I was a child. My own father pounding the pulpit, screaming of damnation and the amens and weeping of
the congregation as the organ played low. This is different but still very
familiar.

It also reminds me of more benevolent times–my first punk rock show,
the pile-ons of kids shouting anthems into the mic, unknown hands
picking me up when I fell down in the mosh pit. How I, a scrawny,
fucked up, kid walked out the doors of shows, with the ammo to fight
for everything I wanted.

I stare into the Clown face and think of Twiztid telling the 'los how
they speak for them, how they're equals. How graciously they gave away
autographs and Star Trek Cereal. I think about the merch booth and the
Juggalos pressed against the chain link fence waiting for the doors to
open. And all around me fat girls become pretty and skinny boys become
tough. Don't fuck with a Juggalo. This night exists for the floobs and
the scrubs. Their night. Faygo pours into their wide-open mouths as the
"WHOOP! WHOOPS!" grow louder and more and more earth-shak-
ing. But I hear them as if underwater, multiple colors of Faygo drenching
me, and I continue to stare into the Clown face as ICP goes into one of
their old school numbers, " I Stuck Her With My Wang".

"I stuck her with my wang, she hit me in the balls, I grabbed her by her
neck and I bounced her off the walls," goes the song. The Juggalos give
up a final WHOOP! WHOOP!

I slip into a sort of hallucinatory state, hearing the Clown laugh in my
head. I wonder how things would be if the Juggalos were given something besides Hatch Gear and Psychopathic Records. I wonder what
would happen if they broke free of the spell of Violent J and Shaggy 2
Dope and grabbed hold of their own power. Would they return to the
Dark Carnival? Would they still be distracted by the prophecies, the wet
T-shirt contests and the Flashlight Wrestling? Would they plant a garden
instead of eating elephant ears and drinking Faygo? Would the trade in

their floob pride for a working class solidarity? Would they wave their hatchets at their oppressors? Would they get an education or simply educate themselves? Would Juggalettes might find less joy in oil-wrestling and the bartering of titty flashes? I look at the Clown and the true shape of its wickedness stares back at me, laughing at me in my state of heightened awareness.

I look down, knowing I let down everyone here who trusted me, everyone who respected me, everyone I befriended by walking out of here and writing this down, talking shit about everything they love and build their lives around. When it comes down to the wire and in spite of, or perhaps because of the Clown Love I receive out here, I'll walk out of Hogrock... and disrespect the Hatchet.

I grow tired, my arms heavy on my shoulders. I think of everyone I knew in the shitty old town of Milltown. I think of friends I left behind, never seeing them again. And how rumors catch up to me, rumors of meth-fueled heart attacks, infanticide, prison sentences for brutal murders. All that resides in the back of my mind somewhere behind a sick, jaded, redneck joke and elitist amnesia. I think of the dispossessed in that town who, indirectly, steered me towards all of this in the first place.

The Clown's smile becomes a sneer that mocks me as the Clown knows I'm onto him, but there's not a goddamn thing that I can do about it. The Clown sneer blinds Violent J and Shaggy from their own detached selves as they search for the power taken from them as children, the false nobility of their prophecy, their vision, their Dark Carnival. The Wicked Clown represents a leadership that leads its followers away from themselves, away from any true unified power. The Clown's face, a pimp of poverty, fear and mental and physical weakness, comes from nothing more than the fallout of triggered post-traumatic stress. I witness the psychopathic lust for power and wealth, and in the face of the Clown, a shocking allegory for humanity itself that we are all bleating sheep, a mass in need of distraction from our struggles. The Clown reveals the mocking face of power and we listen, we follow, and we take on its wicked mask and become hoes to our own fear.

But the show goes on. I think of the Juggalos and their reverence to the power of their mad and mentally-ill leaders, all following a vague watered-down version of Judeo-Christian morality through songs of misogyny and violence. I think of the Juggalos' kindness. Their love of their self-made Family. Their community. I realize the only good things the Juggalos received from their prophets they actually created themselves. They started the Family. They take care of each other. They love each other. They ensure a Juggalo never dies alone, or won't wander of into the woods in the dark and die of an overdose. They always have each others backs. And they did this themselves. Not Violent J and Shaggy. Not the Dark Carnival and not "God." No, the Juggalos actualized the Family without their idols help.

A thunderous WHOOP! WHOOP! brings me back as the stage goes dark and the show ends. The Dark Carnival is God and Insane Clown Posse aren't sorry they tricked us.

The Juggalos chant "FAM-UH-LEE! FAM-UH-LEE!" as they spread out across Hogrock to rage through the rest of the final night.

"Hey ninja, you OK?" a Juggalette asks, leaning over me, shaking me.

I jerk upright.

"Yeah, yeah," I say looking around me in a daze.

"Cool, ninja, I just wanted to make sure you were all right," she says and goes off into the night.

Somewhere in the distance I hear the chanting of "FAM-UH-LEE!" I passed out in a field of trash, to my left the merch tent stands empty of its wares. Next to me lies my yellow backpack containing my camera and empty water bottle. On the other side of me lies an empty bottle of whiskey. I have no recollection how long I laid here. A few Juggalos still mosey around partying, but not many. I get up, pack my stuff up and walk the trail. I walk over the Drug Bridge, and past the Tilt-A-Whirl, and into a big tent where I hear some noise. In this Big Baller tent a 'lette grinds a pole and a DJ pokes at a computer. About ten other people stand in the shadows. The only thing to look at is the young girl languidly twisting around a pole. Everyone is worn out, close to crashing, and trying to get all they can out of the final hours before packing it up and heading home.

"Hey, what's up, ninja? How's it going?" My eyes turn from the dancer and see Gore, the guy who camped near me.

"Just chilling."

"Yeah, me too. You have a good time here?"

"Yeah, man, I did."

We look around the tent, the crowd dwindling down to just a few.

"I'm headin' back to my camp," I say.

"Yeah, I think I'm heading that way, too. I'm tired."

We walk out of the tent, through seas of trash, past the dark and gaping main stage and past the wrestling stage. We walk together in silence, past spray-painted port-a-potties that display "Namaste sharts," past the empty autograph tents, past the merch tent, past the carnival games, past the Tilt-A-Whirl, past the Saturn 6, past the Juggalo jail, and past the seminar tent.

As we reach the exit and pass through it for the last time, I think of Eden. I turn, look back and see no angels with flaming swords guarding the gates of Shangri-la.